TYSON'S GIFT

*How an 8-Pound K9 Became a Man's Greatest
Spiritual Guide*

BRANDON WAINWRIGHT

Edited by Vince Font
Cover design by Christopher Fuzi
Cover design concept by Brandon and Tyson Wainwright
Front cover photo by Dr. Michael McQuary
"Super Tyson" suit by David Wainwright
Rear cover photo by Dublin Creek Kennels
Published by Glass Spider Publishing
www.glassspiderpublishing.com

GLASSSPIDERPUBLISHING

This book is dedicated to the spirit of love for our pets,
who selflessly bring so much joy to the world.

1: A NEW DOG

I am a police officer. A trained observer. Someone who deals in logic and tangible reality on a daily basis. I'm not given to flights of fancy or belief in unbelievable things. In that way, I am and always have been a skeptic. And yet everything I'm about to tell you is true. It happened. It's still happening. And it started the day my girlfriend Misha decided to adopt a dog.

It was July of 2005. Misha and I had hit a rough patch in our relationship. We'd been dating for about a year, and in that time we'd both behaved in ways that triggered our mutual emotional baggage issues.

Misha had decided to put our relationship on hold, although we never really stopped seeing each other. We were just starting to work things out when she called and dropped the news.

She was getting a dog.

I didn't take it well.

Don't get me wrong. I love dogs. Always have. But the last thing I needed was some dog coming between us just as we were starting to work things out. Distracting her from me. What if she *wanted* to be distracted from me? This dog could end up being the embodiment of our relationship's demise!

Of course, I didn't communicate any of these feelings to Misha. The last thing I wanted was for her to think I was so insecure that I'd get jealous over a dog (even if it was true). Plus, it would have been pretty selfish of me to put my foot down. I wanted her to know that I loved and supported her.

His name was Tyson, and he was about a year old. He belonged to Misha's friend Lucy, whose family was moving into a home where they were allowed only one dog. Being the second dog and the newcomer to the family, Tyson had to go. Misha was an obvious choice to adopt because she'd met Tyson before and adored him.

"What kind of dog is he?" I asked.

"He's a Chihuahua-Dachshund mix," Misha replied.

Inside, I lost it. *You've got to be kidding!* I thought. *Come on! A Chihuahua? A yappy little ankle-biter? Couldn't you get a Labrador or a Golden Retriever?*

Outside, I held it together nicely. "Cool!"

"I'm picking him up after work tomorrow."

"I thought you were coming with me to Placerville to visit my mom," I protested.

"Oh, I am. Tyson will just have to come with us."

Oh, boy, I thought. But at least it seemed I was still a priority to Misha. Maybe this dog thing would end up being okay after all. And I really was a dog person. But a *Chihuahua?* After years of residential water delivery, I knew all too well that they weren't particularly friendly animals. Plus, they were always so shaky and nervous. Oh, well. It looked like Misha and Tyson had become a package deal.

2: HE BIT ME!

The next night, Misha arrived at my place around dusk. The plan was to drive up to Placerville to visit my mom for the weekend. The fact that Misha wanted to spend the weekend with me *and* my mom was a big deal as far as I was concerned. It meant she really was serious about our relationship. I didn't think she'd want to spend time with my family otherwise.

She pulled into the driveway in her pickup. I approached her door and she gave me an upbeat kiss hello. She then gestured toward the passenger seat, where a ridiculously cute little dog looked back at me from inside a small crate. He looked like he weighed less than ten pounds.

And he was snarling.

"He bit me," she said.

"What do you mean, he bit you?"

"Oh, he didn't hurt me. He was just scared."

Misha got out of the truck so I could get a closer look at Tyson. I peered in at him. The first thing I noticed was his beautiful multicolored eyes.

"Hey, handsome boy! Look at those beautiful eyes!" I cooed.

Tyson didn't buy it. He snapped and barked at me with such venom that I was taken aback. And a little bit worried. He didn't look scared to me. Nope. He looked pissed.

"Hi, Tyson. I'm Brandon. You don't have to be concerned about me. I'm your friend."

But it was like he hated everything about me. He barked and snarled some more. This was unusual. Dogs had always taken to me.

"Ah, come on, little buddy," I said softly, consolingly.

The venom just kept coming. He seemed to be saying, "Hey, asshole, I don't care who you are! Get lost! I want nothing to do with you *or* this lady who took me from my family!!!"

To tell the truth, I found him kind of comical. He was painfully adorable: brown, with a face that was a perfect blend between Chihuahua and Dachshund. His ears looked like they were on wrong. And he was tiny. But his body didn't match his personality. Tyson had more attitude than any dog I had ever come across. I knew some of that malice had to be driven by fear, but he also had an ample supply of tough-guy confidence.

Without realizing it, I had already begun to respect this little creature.

3: LOVE HER, HATE YOU

On our way up to Placerville, Tyson let Misha hold him in her lap. He wasn't so generous with me. He stared at me distrustfully. If I tried talking to him, he rebuked me with a low growl. If I reached my hand in his general direction, the growl became more pronounced.

We arrived at my mom's late that night. Her dogs, Rudy and Comet, both West Highland Terriers, greeted us at the door. Rudy was a mischievous youngster with a barking problem, so Mom had him wearing a muzzle. He looked like a hilarious combination of Hannibal Lecter and an anteater. His tongue kept poking out of the muzzle as he enthusiastically tried to say hello. Comet, a very distinguished gentleman, greeted us with dignity and a friendly wag of the tail.

Misha set Tyson's crate on the floor and opened the door. He stepped out apprehensively and greeted Comet and Rudy. To our relief, he had no problem mingling with them. He also seemed to already be much more comfortable with Misha. In fact, he seemed to have decided that Misha belonged to *him*. He didn't appear to have a problem with Mom, either. But when it came to me, he wanted nothing to do with it.

Tyson stayed glued to Misha the whole time we were there. This meant that if I got anywhere near Misha, he growled.

Hey, man! I thought. *What's your problem!? We're both lucky to even be in her life! Can't we share?*

Nope. It was clear. Sharing was not an option. I had to accept the fact that I wasn't going to enjoy snuggling with Misha that night. She slept on the couch with Tyson, and I slept on the floor next to them. When I popped up to kiss her goodnight, she held Tyson against her stomach, safely away from our faces. He growled reproachfully.

As the weekend progressed, I attempted to bond with Tyson. I tried to coax him to me, which was met with more growls. I persistently tried to pet him. That only got me bit every time. Although he was fiercely animated about it, he never actually bit down hard. He was just trying to show me he wasn't going to be a soft target.

I found this endearing. I respected his assertive tough-guy attitude, but the fact he made the effort not to hurt me told me there was a sweet dog behind that butthead exterior.

It was abundantly clear that Tyson already loved Misha. Although she was very much enjoying being in his favor, she seemed to enjoy his disdain for me just as much! I'm sure it probably made her feel special to be accepted in such a contrastingly positive manner, and the humor of the situation wasn't lost on either of us.

He was so animated and emotional. With her, Tyson was a sweet little prince. With me, he was a diabolical hellhound! He certainly had strong emotions about us both, and his love for Misha was very much reciprocated. I definitely admired him. But I didn't think it likely that we'd ever become close pals.

4: GETTING CHIPPED

My brother Chason's girlfriend, Alana, is a veterinarian. That Sunday, she invited Misha and Mom to bring Tyson, Rudy, and Comet to her clinic to get microchipped. We'd also noticed that Tyson constantly held his right rear leg up when he walked, so Alana agreed to X-ray his leg.

This was the first time we had ventured out to a public place with Tyson. We were curious to see how he'd do. The clinic catered to animals of all sizes, so in addition to other dogs, there were also horses and goats there. To our surprise, Tyson was surprisingly chill.

We brought our posse of dogs into the exam room to have them injected with electronic microchips. If the dogs ever got lost, any vet or animal rescue with a chip reader could scan the microchip and determine to whom the dogs belonged. The procedure involved injecting the chip into the space between the dog's shoulder blades with an enormous syringe.

Man, I thought, *Tyson is not going to like this.*

Rudy was the first victim, and when Alana pushed the needle in, he yelped loudly.

Tyson was up next. To this day I'm not sure why, but Misha asked me to hold him.

He already hates me, and you want me to hold him while he gets stuck with that needle?! I thought and readied myself. But when Misha placed him in my arms, shockingly, he remained calm.

I couldn't believe it. I was pretty certain he knew what was coming was going to hurt, yet he allowed me to hold him without a fuss. I was truly touched!

I gently rubbed his chest and whispered reassuringly in his ear. As Alana approached with the syringe, I held my breath. I knew Tyson was probably going to go nuts. She injected the chip . . . and he took it.

Tough as nails. No yelp, no nothing. After Rudy's reaction, I wouldn't have been surprised if he'd screamed and bitten us both, but he didn't. He just sat there with dignity. I looked into his eyes as he stared around the room like nothing had happened. I was a proud papa.

Comet, the distinguished gentleman, also handled the procedure with quiet dignity. The situation seemed to elicit the basic personalities of all three dogs. Rudy was the mischievous little kid, Tyson was the tough guy, and Comet was the college professor.

Later, Misha and I joked that if the dogs were smokers, Rudy would prefer candy cigarettes and Comet would smoke a pipe with only the finest tobacco—but Tyson would smoke Pall Mall non-filters.

When Alana took an X-ray of Tyson's rear legs and hips, the results were startling. Compared to the left side, his right hip joint looked practically disintegrated. Rather than showing a smooth ball and socket, the X-ray revealed a jagged, gnarled mass. No wonder he avoided putting weight on it.

Alana couldn't tell if the damage was due to a developmental issue or if Tyson had been injured. Apparently, this type of problem was fairly common, though, and Alana didn't think it would be a big deal to correct.

She told us about a procedure where the hip joint was removed, and cartilage would grow back in its place. The only problem was the cost. Because anesthesia was required, it would run us at least $1000.

Alana offered to do the procedure for free once she had her own practice and anesthesia machine, which she believed would happen very soon. She didn't think Tyson was in a lot of discomfort, so she thought that would be the best route to take. Neither Misha nor I had an extra $1000 lying around, so we agreed to wait.

I decided to focus on the positive results of our trip to the vet. Tyson had his chip, and he'd actually let me hold him. I felt that maybe we had turned a corner. I mean, he had to trust me a little if he was going to let me hold him while he got a shot, right? I had been the only man in the room. Maybe he believed I was protecting him?

I began to realize how important it was to me that Tyson and I became friends. It wasn't just because he was Misha's dog. She seemed to find his hostility toward me humorous anyway, so apparently, I could win the girl without winning the dog. There was just something exceptionally beautiful behind his hostile tough-guy exterior that drew me in.

There was a certain warmth and sweetness about Tyson, especially when Misha was holding him. It was more than just an underlying softness. On a gut level, I knew he longed to feel safe and that he was healing from a past trauma. He wanted to trust me, but he was afraid of me because I was a man.

As far as Misha knew, her coworker Lucy had pampered Tyson, but I believed strongly that there was something in his past. I wanted to help give him a happy, secure life. I didn't realize it at the time, but he was already capturing my heart.

5: THE LEOPARD SEAL

The following Monday night after work, I arrived at Misha's apartment to spend the evening with her. I knocked on the door, and Misha called out from her bedroom for me to come in. But when I stepped inside, Tyson ran out from the bedroom, growling defensively.

I didn't know at first if I was going to get attacked for my troubles, but when he saw it was me, he seemed to relax. I took that as a good sign.

I watched him trot around the living room, his nails clicking on the hardwood floors. Before that, the only places I'd seen him were in Misha's truck, my mom's house, and the vet clinic. In all three places, Tyson had stayed glued to Misha, so it was cool to see him trotting around the apartment like he owned the place. He seemed much more normal as opposed to the holy terror I'd met over the weekend.

"Hey, Tyson! How are you, little buddy?" I offered enthusiastically.

He stopped trotting around and looked at me aloofly.

"Come on over here, little dude!" I coaxed.

The answer was no. He turned around dismissively and clicked back into Misha's room.

We took him for a walk and got burritos at the taqueria up the road. Misha and I were very much enjoying each other's company, and Tyson seemed to be pretty happy too. He stopped at every bush to sniff it thoroughly, followed by a quick spray to mark his territory.

As we settled in to watch *Law and Order* reruns, which had become our nightly custom, Tyson curled up in Misha's lap.

He hadn't allowed me to hold him since the vet, but he'd done well with me holding his leash. He wasn't super friendly toward me, but he wasn't overtly hostile, either. I decided to try petting him.

I extended my hand and gently rubbed his head. He actually allowed it! He watched me *very* apprehensively, but he allowed it.

I ended up spending the night at Misha's, and when I got into bed and lay on my back, Misha brought Tyson up on the bed. I figured he'd stay as far from me as possible, but to my utter shock, he jumped onto my chest and started licking my face.

Wow! I thought. *I guess we're buds now!*

That was when I went to rub his ears and found out that we weren't buds yet. He ran away from me so quickly that I thought he was going to fly off the bed. I put my arms under the covers so he wouldn't feel threatened and tried to lure him back to me.

"Come on, Tyson. Gimme kisses!"

Moving slowly, he crept closer, climbed onto my chest, and picked up where he left off. I lay there as passively as I could while Tyson licked my face.

Misha was amazed. "Wow," she said. "Does he like you, or is he trying to show dominance?"

The licking went on and on and on. About five minutes later, he finally got tired and stopped. Then he curled up with Misha and went to sleep.

What a peculiar little dog, I thought. *But hey, I'll take it. At least we're friends now.*

The next morning, I left for work before sunup. Misha and Tyson were still asleep, so I came into the bedroom and kissed Misha goodbye. I looked down at Tyson. His eyes were open and he was staring up at me from behind Misha.

I thought, *We're friends now. I'll kiss you goodbye too!*

As I brought my head down, he snapped at me. He wasn't trying to bite me. It was more of a warning. Clearly, we weren't friends yet.

March of the Penguins, a documentary about emperor penguins in Antarctica, was out in movie theaters, and Misha and I had seen it about a week prior. In the movie, there is a shot where a leopard seal (the penguins' main predator) swims upward and snaps at the camera as it attacks a penguin. The result is that the viewer gets to see the attack from the point of view of the penguin.

When Tyson snapped at me that day, it was just like the scene in the movie—and from that point on, one of his most endearing nicknames became "The Leopard Seal."

6: DO YOU BEAT HIM OR SOMETHING?

Misha lived in a small apartment complex with only four units, one of which was occupied by her landlord, Bernie. He was a really nice guy and a very fair landlord, but he had a strict policy about dogs. They were prohibited. Slight problem.

When Misha informed him about Tyson and asked if he would consider allowing him to stay, Bernie's reply was absolute. "That's a request I can't grant."

With that, Misha began looking for a new apartment. She found one just up the road. It was reasonably priced (something you'll never see again in Menlo Park, California) and about twice the size of Bernie's, with two bedrooms and two bathrooms. Score!

We moved her and Tyson in a week later. Little did I know, I was also moving in. After that, I never spent another night at my own place.

Misha and I were still working through the rough patch, but we were making progress. The walls were rapidly coming down, and the new apartment felt like a symbol for the fresh start we were committed to. Tyson was already having a positive impact on our relationship. He was helping us create a new chapter.

Upon moving in, Misha wanted to get some new pillows for her bed, so, along with Tyson, we walked to a nearby mattress store. Misha carried Tyson in her arms like a baby as we looked around. When she found a therapeutic pillow she was looking for, she wanted to try it out, so she went to hand Tyson to me.

By now Tyson was used to me, but he was still pretty skittish around me. He never let me pick him up, and the only way to coax him to me was to lay down to eye-level with him.

That being said, one of his favorite things to do was to lick my face relentlessly every night at bedtime. He had already let me hold him once at the vet, so I figured he'd be okay with me holding him while Misha tested her pillow.

Boy, was I wrong! She went to hand him to me, and he went nuts. He panicked and squealed like he was going to the slaughter. He bit at my hands like a little shrew—only he didn't actually bite hard. He was just afraid, and he wanted me to know he was a fighter.

I laughed, but not mockingly. It was endearing. I pulled him into my chest and held him while he calmly stared up at me. I rubbed his head reassuringly.

"What's up with you, you crazy little dog?" I asked, but he didn't answer.

As we stood there bonding, I locked eyes with two women standing a few feet away. They glared at me with judgment and unmistakable contempt. They seemed to be thinking, *That little dog would never react that way unless you were abusing him. Do you beat him or something?*

I just smiled pleasantly. They continued to glare.

Oh, go pound sand, I thought.

What mattered most to me at that moment was how relaxed Tyson was in my arms. He didn't try to squirm away. He didn't continue to bite. He didn't even tense up. He just relaxed and settled in. This seemed to be his true nature—at least when he didn't feel threatened.

He was turning out to be a really sweet dog. With Misha, he was an absolute lover, a total snuggle-bug. He was still apprehensive with me, even when I lay on my back, but he was also a prolific giver of kisses (something we lovingly referred to as "licky-licky"). He was the most high-maintenance dog I'd ever met, sure, but he was anything but mean.

I was really beginning to form a connection with him. He was complicated, but he was beautiful. He was like a little person—a fur person.

As we walked home with Misha's bounty of new pillows, I felt truly blessed; blessed to be in the life of my true love, and blessed to be in the life of this beautiful but complicated little dog.

7: A PROPOSAL

About a week after we moved into the new apartment, all remnants of the "rough patch" seemed to disappear. Misha and I both had to face significant fears in order to work things out. Frankly, I hadn't really given her my heart until she broke up with me and I was faced with losing her forever.

Before the breakup, I had loved Misha, and I knew instinctively that she was the right woman for me. It just took me some time to get there. Finally, I had been ready and willing to give it my all. The only problem? She wasn't having it.

By the time I had gotten myself together, Misha had shut down emotionally. At first, I felt betrayed. Opening up was one of the hardest things I'd ever done, and it hurt to have that door slammed in my face. But I knew her pulling away was a natural reaction. I also knew that if I had any chance of getting her back, I was going to have to eat shit for a while.

Fortunately, she never stopped agreeing to see me and I never stopped agreeing to be fed humble pie. Misha put me through the wringer for what seemed like an eternity but was really about two months. Toward the end, I really began to think I'd lost her.

I felt like an ass. I had found an amazing, beautiful woman who had opened her heart to me, and I had ruined it. Groveling felt horrible, but I knew I had it coming. A very trusted confidant was appalled by my willingness to put up with her icy behavior, and he told me to run like hell. But I knew I had to earn her trust back. The only way to do that was to show her that I loved her enough to work through it.

Fortunately, her mom, Diane, came to my rescue. She was my savior. Just when I was ready to cut my losses and walk away, Diane talked me into not giving up. Just as importantly, she also gave some very sage advice: "Don't call Misha for a couple of weeks." She was sure Misha just needed some time to reflect and that she'd come around before I knew it.

What did I have to lose? It was torture, but I didn't communicate with her for two weeks. Eventually, she called me and we agreed to meet for dinner.

I was scared to death I was going to screw things up again, but Diane was right. Slowly, Misha and I began to work things out. Soon after, Tyson came into our lives and Misha got the new apartment. The relationship began to flourish.

Ever since the beginning, I'd known Misha was the right woman for me. I just wasn't able to allow myself to feel safe—ironic, because so many times in the past I'd felt safe when I really shouldn't have. Now I felt more comfortable letting my guard down. Despite the hurt we had both experienced, we had remained true to one another, and that meant everything.

I saw no reason to wait around. Within a couple of weeks of moving into the new apartment, I took swift action.

With the help of my good buddy Eric and his wife, Kate, a table and chairs were pre-staged on the beach at Point Reyes National Seashore. Misha and I went for a walk on the beach. I pretended to stumble on the scene, which was tucked away in some seagrass near the bluffs.

"Huh," I said. "Looks like someone left us some cheese and wine. I guess we should enjoy it!"

The engagement ring I'd bought her was hidden in my wine glass, so it didn't take me long to get to the point of the occasion. I took the ring out, got on one knee, and asked her to marry me. Without hesitation, she accepted, and I felt a love and a peace I'll never forget. To this day, I still feel it.

Unfortunately, Tyson couldn't be there for the proposal, although

I certainly thought of him and hoped he would approve. Whether he wanted it or not, I was now his dad.

8: A TURNING POINT

The next few months of our lives were euphoric. The wedding wouldn't happen until the following May, but that really felt like a technicality. We created a home together, and I felt a love and peace I hadn't allowed myself to experience since before my parents divorced when I was fourteen (I was now thirty-two).

Tyson was slowly becoming more comfortable with me. He continued his nightly ritual of "licky-licky," after which he'd curl up with Misha and fall fast asleep. Whenever Misha and I sat on the couch, he'd hop into her lap and allow me to pet him. He was always willing to commune with me a bit, but only as long as I lay on the ground. Otherwise, he had to be with Misha.

We were bonding, albeit slowly. His interactions with me always took place under limited conditions, but he was becoming less guarded. As I was the only man he would allow to get anywhere near him without a fuss, I felt special. I was becoming a part of his inner circle.

I've known some wonderful dogs who were friendly with just about everyone, but their friendliness didn't always feel very personal. With Tyson, it was. Any warmth and connection I enjoyed with him was the result of his deliberate decision to allow it, and it was very special to me.

I could sense that his opening up to me was a cathartic process for him as well. Whatever had conditioned him to be so defensive around me—and all other men, for that matter—had left quite a mark. Our relationship was helping him to heal, and it was doing both of our souls a lot of good.

Tyson was a prolific food scavenger, constantly patrolling for droppings of any kind. He liked vegetables, junk food, pretty much anything. He didn't care about getting in trouble for it, either. If you made the mistake of leaving food where he could get to it, he'd swiftly steal it.

The good thing about his passion for food was that he quickly forgot all about his fears. If you had food, he'd come right over to you and wait for you to drop something on the floor. I started using this to my advantage, offering him nibbles from my plate. Not enough to make a nutritional impact, but enough to get him to hang out with me and allow us to bond more.

About a month and a half after Misha and I were engaged, she took Tyson to a social gathering, where his lust for food became detrimental to his health. His former mama, Lucy, was there, and they were very happy to see each other. While Misha mingled with friends, Tyson visited with Lucy, who displayed her love for him by showering him with treats from the snack table. Not a good idea. This gave him a bad case of indigestion and gas.

I'm sure by now it's more than clear Tyson was a very emotional dog, very expressive. Sure, he demonstrated his apprehension around me, but his expressiveness transcended the gamut of emotions. If he was sad, you could see it in his face. The same if he was angry. It was written on his face. You could actually see the emotion in his eyes. If he was feeling loving, you could see that as well—just as you could see his happiness, which was of course always accompanied by the frenzied wagging of his tail.

By the time Misha and Tyson got home from the party, Tyson was feeling sick. You could see it in the way he lay curled in a ball, lethargic and miserable. He was so miserable, in fact, that he didn't even have the energy to avoid me or resist me when I came near him.

I realized this was my chance to solidify some trust between us. I curled up with him, pulling him into my chest so I could wrap him up in a protective cocoon. I gently stroked his fur and told him I was sorry he wasn't feeling well, but that I'd stay right there with him until he felt better.

He actually seemed to soak this up. So did I. And while I enjoyed the opportunity to comfort him and snuggle with him, I was also hoping my protecting him while he was feeling vulnerable would make a significant impact.

Tyson was still miserable when we went to bed. I could hear the sound of gas bubbles gurgling inside him. He looked at me helplessly. I felt so bad for him.

"Aww, little buddy," I said, trying to comfort him. "This will pass soon." I curled up with him, and we all fell asleep.

At some point, Tyson got up and jumped off the bed. Soon, Misha and I were awakened by a gnarly smell coming from the foot of the bed.

"I think he farted," she said.

"That's no fart!" I gasped.

Simultaneously, we jumped out of bed to check on him. Sure enough, it was no fart. There was a large puddle of diarrhea on the floor.

In my experience, most dogs would show shame or embarrassment in this situation. Not Tyson. As I said, he was like a little person. He looked at us without shame. He felt awful, and that was all he cared about.

"Poor guy," we both lamented.

We giggled as we cleaned up the mess and tucked him back in bed. He stared up at us with a look of judgment that said his discomfort was *our* fault. This just made us giggle more. He didn't seem to appreciate our laughter, but he was all good with me curling up with him again.

I hoped he and I had turned a corner, and that he would allow me to get closer to him even after he'd regained his strength. I would soon find out.

9: A NEW DAY

Tyson felt much better the next day. But not everything went back to normal. Things had changed. Things between him and me.

Apparently, all the nurturing I'd provided to him *did* mean something to him, because suddenly I was able to pick him up without having him freak out.

He started sitting with me on the couch, even when Misha was around. If Misha and I snuggled together, Tyson would sit across both of our laps. Often, when Misha and I would hug we'd do it with Tyson between us. We called this "the circle of love."

I started taking Tyson with me everywhere I went. If I left him in the car, he would always greet my return by jumping up, putting his paws on the armrest, and pressing his face against the window. Sometimes, when I got home from work, he'd run around the apartment at full speed to celebrate my arrival. This was pure sunshine for my soul.

I know what you're thinking. This all sounds like typical behavior, the kind of antics enjoyed between a dog and their human. But it meant the world to me, especially since it had been so hard-earned. As I've said, Tyson was like a little person; a very emotional, expressive fur person. It was like getting to know and establish trust with a needy, guarded child.

In the beginning, his discomfort with me had been palpable. It wasn't just him being a pugnacious asshole. I really believed there had been significant trauma in his past. As we grew closer, our relationship was helping him to heal, and it warmed my heart.

Before long, the only things that made him skittish were sudden, loud noises or interacting with men other than me. That said, his neediness didn't diminish in the least. As Misha liked to say, "Tyson's needs are many, and they are frequent."

If he wanted to be left alone and you tried petting him or getting in his space, he'd look up at you with a look of utter irritation. Either that or he'd just keep his head down and growl softly.

If he wanted to sit on your lap, he'd jump up on you or yelp until you picked him up. If you went anywhere without him, he'd look at you with such sadness that it melted your heart. If he was hungry, he'd bark until you fed him. If he had to pee, he'd sit at the door and stare at you until you let him out or took him for a walk. Tyson wanted what he wanted *when* he wanted it, and he wasn't afraid to show it!

If you got mad at him and raised your voice—more often than not for swiping food without permission—he didn't seem to care. Needless to say, swatting him with a newspaper wasn't an option because he'd surely be traumatized. But if you gave him the cold shoulder, he'd follow you around with such sadness that you'd think his best friend had died. This was, without doubt, his most effective punishment.

For all of his demanding, emotional quirkiness, Tyson had a level of affection I'd never experienced in an animal. He'd sit in your lap and look back at you (not by turning his head, but rather by looking up higher and higher until you came into his view) with the softest eyes, an expression of total affection. As long as he was with me and Misha, his pack was together and he was happy and content. Tyson was mischievous, self-serving, demanding, and absolutely loving.

His quirkiness even extended to the way he wagged his tail, which he did more than ever now that he was completely happy in his surroundings. Rather than wagging it in a normal horizontal motion, he wagged it vertically. It was peculiar, but it added to his unique personality. Sometimes we endearingly referred to him as "the vertical tail-wagger."

As time wore on, his nightly ritual of "licky-licky" became more enthusiastic. Not only would Tyson stand on my chest and lick me relentlessly, but now if I tried to stop him by pulling him away, he'd just charge back over and pick up where he left off.

Sometimes it drove Misha nuts. Not because he was giving me his attention, but because his licking sessions were so loud. I didn't mind it. I was the center of the affection and I would return the favor by rubbing his ears and communing with him. It wasn't so much fun for Misha, who'd sometimes get frustrated and yell at us like we were obnoxious kids.

"Geez, you guys are so loud!"

Tyson was not deterred. Usually, it took one of us grabbing him and curling up with him, or me laying him on his back with his head on my chest or shoulder, to get him to stop. Even then, it always took several attempts.

Eventually, the standard evening ritual became: 1) "licky-licky"; 2) Tyson falling asleep on my chest or shoulder; 3) and Tyson migrating behind Misha's legs as she lay on her side. This is where he stayed until morning. It was a pattern that continued for the rest of his life.

10: THE BOBO

By October (three months after Tyson came into our lives and one month after he and I had finally bonded), I was absolutely in love with that dog, and so was Misha. He was our little fur child. Even at the time, I realized how immensely he contributed to the foundation of love and cohesion upon which our life and marriage were being built. Misha and I loved and nurtured him together, and this brought us closer.

Tyson opened our hearts with his spunky, sensitive, demanding personality, and this helped our hearts to grow and evolve together. We understood on an instinctive, spiritual level that he was in our lives for a reason. We also understood it was important to appreciate every day with him.

One night, I was on the living room couch and Misha was in the kitchen with Tyson. Suddenly, I heard Misha yell, "No, Bobo, no!"

I went into the kitchen to see what was going on. Misha was trying to cook dinner, but Tyson was running around the kitchen, jumping up onto her legs, being his general goofy self.

"Bobo?" I said.

"Well," Misha said, "earlier I looked down at him, and I just knew his nickname was Bobo."

That was it. For the rest of Tyson's life, we called him "Bobo." Or, when it felt right, "The Bobo." It was a name we wound up using more often than his actual name. To this day, Misha is convinced Tyson had somehow communicated that nickname to her. Who's to say? Maybe he did.

Misha and her Bobo.

11: HEARTLIGHT

Not long after we started calling him Bobo, we decided to have a portrait of Tyson created. Misha had a coworker who was an artist, and the plan was to take a photograph of Tyson and print it onto canvas. Then the artist would paint the canvas to create a sort of painting/photo hybrid.

Misha and her artist friend held a quick photo shoot with Tyson during their lunch break. To hear them tell it, Tyson was a little nightmare, and anything but cooperative—running all over the place, rolling around in the grass, and generally refusing to sit still.

Despite this, they managed to get one good shot of him holding in place and appearing mellow. The painting turned out great, and we still have it on display on an easel in our home.

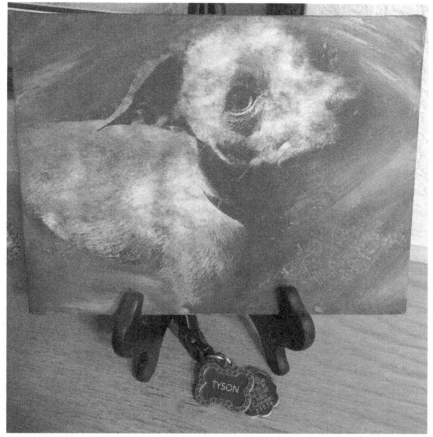

Tyson's portrait, which we now call "Heartlight."

The rest of the photos were unusable but still adorable, so I took copies of them to work with me and attached them to the wall on the inside of my DHL delivery truck. Those photos warmed my heart, especially when I was having a bad day.

One afternoon, I was taking a break between deliveries and pickups in a parking lot on my route when Tyson's former mama, Lucy, pulled up alongside me. She was no longer working with Misha, and she wanted to find out how Tyson was doing.

As you can probably imagine, being the proud papa I was, I gushed about how much we loved him and how much joy he had brought us.

I bragged about how close he and I had grown, and I showed her the pictures I had on display.

I could tell it gave her great joy to see he was so loved and that he loved us in return. I hoped it eased any feelings of guilt she may have had over giving him up. I assured her she was welcome to visit with him anytime she wanted.

As Lucy drove off, I sat there contemplating how lucky we were to have Tyson in our lives. Not only was he helping Misha and me grow closer, but he was also opening my heart in a way I hadn't experienced since I was a child. I may have been a 32-year-old man, but Tyson was connecting to and healing the young boy in me.

Not that my growing up was terrible. I had a pretty good childhood. I had a mom and dad who loved me, a younger brother and sister, and we lived in a decent neighborhood. I had many friends, I played sports, and I was a Cub Scout. We didn't have much money, but we weren't poor. I had several paper routes, as well as a robust lawn mowing business. We lived near a wooded park, and I enjoyed many fun-filled days of running through the woods and playing by the creek. That said, like most kids, I was no stranger to animal-related traumas.

When I was very young, we got a white terrier mix named Skampy—Skamp for short. He probably weighed thirty pounds. He was a sweet, gentle dog. You could climb all over him and he'd just roll with it. He was great about never going potty in the house, and he was always there to cuddle if you needed it.

The only problem with Skamp was that he had ear mites. This caused his ears to smell horrible, and the only way to keep that at bay was to take him to the groomer once a month to have his ears (and the rest of him) trimmed. They also treated his ears with medicated soap.

His care was expensive, and my parents didn't have a lot to spend. It became an issue. One morning when I was about eight years old, my parents got into an argument about Skamp—and my dad threatened to give him away.

I was absolutely devastated. I went to school crying, and I was sad all day long. Skamp was a part of our family, and I loved him with all my heart. The idea that we could send him away seemed impossibly cruel. He was just an innocent dog, and now his whole life was in jeopardy because of Dad's frustration. Skamp deserved better.

But my father wasn't a cruel person, and when I got home from school that day I was relieved to learn he'd changed his mind. Still, the heartbreak of a whole day spent grieving over the possibility of losing Skamp left its mark. Looking back, I think it hardened me a bit emotionally.

Although we kept Skamp, my parents didn't take him to the groomers for much longer. Soon he became a shaggy, smelly mess. No one, not even me, would go anywhere near him, and the poor guy just sat on our back porch all day being ignored. When my friends came over, they'd make fun of how smelly he was. Eventually, when I was ten, my dad decided it wasn't right for him to live like that. But rather than take him to the groomers again, he took Skamp to the animal shelter and gave him up.

Needless to say, I was sad about the whole thing, but not as sad as I should have been. I was just as guilty as everyone else of ignoring Skamp. Yeah, I cried when my dad took him away, but I could have done more for him. I was a dumb kid, and I didn't pay attention to how awful Skamp's life had become until Dad decided it was time for him to go. I should have, but I didn't.

To this day, Dad regrets how he handled the situation. He is still haunted by the way Skamp looked at him when the door to the kennel at the shelter was closed. I'm confident that if he could do things over again, Dad would figure out a way to pay for the groomers.

Part of the problem was that my mom had a habit of bringing home animals without consulting Dad first. She had done this several times before Skamp came along, although I was too young to remember. Other than the ear mites, Skamp was a great dog, but the other dogs and cats apparently had behavioral issues.

Unfortunately, Mom didn't put much effort into training them, and Dad always ended up repairing things they destroyed or going to the animal shelter to pick them up after they ran away. He would always protest, but Mom seemed not to hear.

About a year after Skamp went to the shelter, Mom brought home another puppy. Her name was Trixie, and I was there the day Mom picked her out. Once again, Dad wasn't included in the decision. At the time, I had no idea of the frustration he was experiencing with regard to Mom and the pets—not that it would have kept me from encouraging her to adopt her.

Trixie was small, probably no more than ten pounds, with a black-and-white coat decorated by touches of brown. She might have been a Jack Russell-Chihuahua mix. Or maybe a Dachshund. I didn't know, and I didn't care. She was cute and sweet, and that was all that mattered to me.

All Trixie wanted to do was play and be close to us. When I got home from school, she'd always be waiting for me at the front door. I'd pick her up and she'd lick me to death, practically going into convulsions with excitement. She was a beautiful soul.

She was a well-behaved dog, too. The only problem she had was that she'd roll over and pee every time Dad walked into the room. She was scared to death of him. He was the alpha, and she was submitting to him. It really shouldn't have been a big deal, but unfortunately, it was. Dad was an interior designer, and he just so happened to be remodeling our house at the time of these incidents. He was not willing to tolerate a dog peeing all over the place.

He put up with it for a while, hoping the issue would take care of itself as Trixie grew older. Of course, it didn't. The catch was, the only person who could have helped Trixie get over her fear of Dad was Dad himself, and he had no interest in her. I didn't know why, but I'm sure it had a lot to do with his irritation over Mom's pet issues.

We probably had Trixie for eight months before Dad decided it was time for her to go. He let us know two weeks in advance, probably as a way of giving us one last opportunity to get her to stop peeing all over the house. I was devastated. She was my innocent little friend, and I loved her so much. I had no idea how to make her break that habit, so I was going to lose her.

For the next two weeks, I constantly worried about her and hoped Dad would change his mind as he had about Skampy the first time.

At the time, "We Are the World" by U.S.A. for Africa was a very popular song. I remember cuddling with Trixie as I fell asleep listening to it on my clock radio. The song was about people helping people. It seemed ironic that so many people wanted to help others, but Dad, who was a very decent man, was so willing to cast our sweet little dog out. It was so unfair that she was going to be abandoned by her humans. I was heartbroken.

Mom didn't do anything about it. She didn't seek out training for Trixie, or anything else for that matter. This followed her normal pattern. Trixie had been dealt a horrible hand, and I cursed the day we brought her home from the pet store. I believed that if we hadn't, another family would have come along and given her a great life. I worried if they took her to the pound she would be euthanized before she was adopted. It was agonizing.

After the two weeks, Dad took her to the pound. It was every bit as horrible as I had dreaded. For days, I tried to just carry on with life as normal, but I was in a state of grief, and the pain was intense. I couldn't hide my despair. I cried a lot and sank into a state of depression.

One night, I overheard Mom telling Dad that he needed to talk to me. He sounded surprised to learn I was still having trouble with the situation, which in turn surprised me—he was normally attentive to me and my siblings. I wondered if his guilt had subconsciously blocked my grief out.

I was on the edge of my bed sobbing when Dad came into my room. He asked me if I was still sad about Trixie. When I told him that I was, he sat down next to me and did his best to comfort me.

When I expressed my concerns about Trixie's fate, he assured me there was no way a cute little dog like her wasn't going to be adopted. He painted the picture of a nice elderly lady adopting her and giving her a great life, and he said he would have been surprised if she hadn't already been adopted.

I had a lot of confidence and trust in him, so this made me feel much better. The more I thought about it, the more likely his assessment seemed. She was still a very young dog, and she *was* so cute and sweet that it was unimaginable anyone wouldn't adopt her.

I let Dad's words give me the comfort and the hope I needed to get through my grief, but I never learned how things turned out for Trixie.

Most people might read this and think my father was cold and unfeeling, but he wasn't. He was and still is a very warm, nurturing parent. Given Mom's history with pets, I think he really believed the decisions he made concerning Skamp and Trixie were the right ones—and at the time, in a way, they were.

These days, most people I know consider their pets to be a part of their family, but thirty-five years ago this wasn't as common. Sure, people have always loved their pets, but not to the same degree they do today.

When I was fourteen, only a couple of weeks into my freshman year of high school, Dad asked Mom for a divorce. This was a huge shock to everyone, including Mom. They rarely fought, so their problems weren't apparent.

Knowing what I know about the relationship now, Mom was simply ignoring their problems. If Dad tried to address them, Mom would take it as an attack and lash out. Dad learned very quickly that the best way to keep the peace was to just try his best to live with their problems. Eventually, he couldn't do it anymore.

I love my mom, and I can honestly say that she is a good person, but she is extremely dysfunctional. When Dad left, she refused to accept it. She was unwilling or unable to honestly look at their relationship and each of their roles in it. She blamed him for everything (and still does). Unfortunately, once Dad left, I was the closest thing to an adult in the house, and Mom used me as a sounding board. She didn't hold back, either.

She badmouthed Dad on a daily basis, and it was horrible. I had (and still have) great respect for him, and I just wasn't willing to accept the awful things she said about him. Especially when I knew they weren't true. So I defended him.

Yeah, it would have been better to either walk away or listen in silence. Eventually, I learned to do this, but at fourteen, I didn't have the wisdom or the maturity to do so. I didn't want to fight with Mom, but she saw my defense of him as an attack on her.

Mom and I had never gotten along very well. Dad had always played the mediator, but now he wasn't there anymore. Mom was barely keeping it together, and she continued to lash out. This resulted in daily verbal brawls between the two of us.

Our household grew miserable, and we were all looking for things to be happy about. So what did we do? Yep, we got another dog.

Sox was a little spitfire, full of feisty puppy energy. We got him from an animal shelter, and they weren't sure what breed he was. He weighed about twenty pounds and we figured he was most likely a Beagle-Boxer mix.

We called him Sox because he was tan all over except for his feet, which were white. Like all puppies, Sox demanded an enormous amount of attention. I played with him a lot, but I didn't really know how to train him properly.

Mom, as she did with all of her other dogs, expected Sox to train himself. Unfortunately, Sox was too intelligent for his own good. When we wanted him to stay in the backyard, we had to lock the deadbolt on the door because he figured out how to turn the knob and let himself in.

He was a prolific chewer, but he especially liked to chew Mom's things. His favorite thing of hers to chew were her eyeglasses. Naturally, Mom made this easy for him by leaving them on her nightstand where Sox could easily get to them and destroy them. He did this to at least three pairs. I've often wondered if the reason Sox targeted Mom's belongings was because of her constant hostility.

Three or four months after we adopted Sox, things between me and Mom got so bad that I went to live with Dad. He had a one-bedroom apartment about five miles away—a distance that at the time seemed very far.

It was a lonely time for me. Although I went to the same high school, all of my friends lived far away from Dad's. He did his best to make it comfortable for me by giving me the bedroom and sleeping on the couch, but I still missed home. Especially my friends and Sox.

The following summer, I talked my parents into letting me move back home. At first, it was a relief. I was so happy to be in my normal stomping grounds and be able to spend time with Sox and my friends. In the beginning, things were even better with Mom.

Of course, Sox's behavioral issues had still not been addressed. Mom soon began to consider him more and more of a nuisance. We never did get him formal training, which would have helped greatly, and over the next few months, he continued to chew things up. Regardless, I loved him a lot. I would take him running with me in the evenings, which he really enjoyed, and at night we would snuggle.

One of my fondest memories with Sox, albeit a sad one, was when he had an allergic reaction and broke out in hives. I was at school at the time, and I suddenly felt extremely ill with flu-like symptoms. I came home with the intent of going straight to bed, but when I found Sox broken out in golf-ball-size hives, I couldn't leave him to his misery.

So I did the only thing I could think of to do. I curled up alongside him and fell asleep, hoping we'd both be okay when we woke up. That was exactly what happened. A couple of hours later, the two of us woke up, totally symptom-free. We had been each other's healer.

It didn't take long for things between me and Mom to deteriorate, and pretty soon we were back to our daily fights. Midway through my sophomore year, I moved back in with Dad. It was a sad time, but it was also a relief to be in a stable environment. The only bad thing was that once again I was far from my friends, my siblings, and Sox. I felt bad not being around to stick up for him as Mom's frustration with him grew.

One day when I was visiting Mom, my Aunt Chris stopped by. She told me that if I didn't get Sox under control, she was going to "take him for a ride." I was furious with her, but even more so with Mom.

It was obvious Mom had been bellyaching to Chris about what a bad dog Sox was and how she was the victim of this horrible creature.

He was just an innocent dog. It was our fault for not training him better. Still, Mom and Chris were serious about taking him to the pound. It was happening again. Another dog was going to be abandoned by us.

I felt that somehow I needed to train him to be better behaved. The problem was that I didn't have a clue how to do it. Plus, I didn't even live with him anymore.

One day, a friend of mine who just so happened to have a well-behaved dog came by while I was at Mom's. I told him all about what was going on and that I had to train Sox quickly or I was going to lose him.

My friend didn't know how to train a dog any more than I did, and he advised me to spank Sox when he misbehaved. I figured since his dog was so well-behaved, he must know what he was talking about. I had never spanked Sox before, and I hated the idea of hitting him, but time was running out and I was desperate.

I started physically disciplining Sox every time he misbehaved. Of course, this only made things worse. His behavior didn't improve at all, and to make matters worse he became afraid of me. One time when I got to Mom's and couldn't find Sox, I looked and found him cowering under the patio deck, shaking. It broke my heart to see him that way.

I gently coaxed him out and held him, petting him softly and reassuring him that he was okay. I felt like a monster, and rightfully so. How could I have been so stupid? What did I expect was going to happen when I spanked him every time I was around him? I hadn't physically injured him, but I had certainly traumatized him. To this day, I still tear up when I think about it. The next time I visited Mom, Sox was gone. She had taken him to the pound.

I was disgusted and sad, but I was also numb. I felt as if I'd lost all respect for Mom. Ultimately, I simply accepted the situation. What else could I do?

Two years later, during my senior year in high school, Mom adopted yet another dog. Victoria was a sweet little West Highland Terrier. She was one of the most adorable things I'd ever seen, but I was furious. I was incensed that Mom had actually brought another innocent destined to be abandoned into her life. I wanted nothing to do with Victoria.

Luckily for her, she had no behavioral issues. No, Mom didn't put any work into her. She was just a good dog by nature. Unfortunately, she had a horrible hereditary skin disease that forced Mom to euthanize her when she was still very young.

I felt bad for her, as well as for Mom and my little sister, Andrea, but it didn't affect me all that much. I had never opened my heart to her.

Throughout my twenties and into my thirties, I remained a dog lover, but the thought of having a dog of my own never crossed my mind. My childhood dog experiences had scarred me, and I just wasn't interested. Not until Tyson.

Tyson opened my heart in much the same way my relationship with Misha helped me heal the trauma of my parents' divorce and the disintegration of my childhood family. On my own, I never would have volunteered to adopt Tyson, but I had adopted him nonetheless. For the first time since I was a kid, I was in a situation where I felt comfortable and open enough to truly connect with a dog.

I didn't even realize it was happening. Tyson was a real pistol; one tough egg to crack. I know now this was a big part of why we connected and why I began to love him so much. In order for me to win his heart and trust, I had to open my heart to him. He wouldn't have had it any other way. I had to connect with the beautiful soul that was behind that tough, nasty facade.

As I sat there in my DHL truck, thankful for Tyson and for the opportunity to express that thanks to Lucy, I heard a song in my head that I hadn't heard in years. "Heartlight" by Neil Diamond. It was a song inspired by the movie *E.T. the Extra-Terrestrial*, and it perfectly captures the warmth and beauty of the relationship between Elliott and

E.T. They were each other's friend, protector, and soul mate. As corny as this may sound, I felt then—and still feel—the same about Tyson. He is my heartlight.

12: I'D TAKE A BULLET FOR YOU, LITTLE BUDDY

One weekend, we went to Dad's and my stepmom Carla's house for dinner. Tyson came along. We were running late, so I ran to our apartment parking lot and pulled the car up to the street to save time. Our apartment was on a moderately busy street.

When I drove up, I saw Tyson emerging from the apartment onto the sidewalk. He wasn't wearing a leash, and Misha was nowhere in sight! It scared me. I was worried he might walk out into the street into the path of traffic.

Fortunately, Misha wasn't far behind, and she called out to him. When he heard her voice, he looked back at her and stopped obediently in his tracks. I was relieved. Although he was a smart dog, sometimes he only stopped and came to you when he was good and ready. Apparently, that only pertained to when he was in his own space.

On this occasion, he clearly sensed the potential dangers of the busy street and took the obedient approach for his own safety. That vertical tail of his was going at high velocity, and he walked in circles of palpable excitement.

What struck me about this scene wasn't just the intelligence he showed by obeying Misha, but the sweet puppy innocence he displayed. When he was in the familiar environment of our apartment, he was sweet but he was also in charge. We were there to maintain the space and take care of him. He loved and adored us, but *he* was master of his own destiny.

As he frolicked excitedly on the sidewalk, his alpha personality transformed into vulnerable innocence. He looked up at Misha as if to say, "Mom, I'm stoked to be out here among all these stimuli, but I need you! I need you to protect me and help me enjoy it safely."

I was so touched; it melted my heart.

I know it probably sounds like an overreaction to such a simple moment, but realize that Tyson was still a tough guy. At least that was the general vibe he gave off. Yes, I had found my way into his heart, and he into mine. Yes, we were very close—but he was still a tough cookie with a tough exterior.

That brief moment in front of the apartment gave me a glimpse at the soft innocence I instinctively knew was there. It was touching to see it, and I felt an almost overwhelming sense of protectiveness toward him.

I'd take a bullet for you, little buddy, I thought. I never stopped feeling that way.

13: THERE'S A TURD IN MY CLOSET!

When we arrived at Dad and Carla's, their Toy Poodle, Frisbee, greeted us at the door. Yep, Dad had another dog in his life. Carla had unexpectedly brought him home one day in the fall of 1993, and, as you'd expect, Dad was less than pleased. He assumed things would go with Frisbee the same way they had gone with Mom's dogs. Fortunately, he was wrong.

Carla trained Frisbee with enthusiasm, and he even won awards at local dog shows. Frisbee was very smart, unbelievably cute, and a real sweetheart. It didn't take long for Dad to fall in love with him. He treated Frisbee like a child, often holding him and loving him adoringly. Dad even had a framed picture of him on the wall in his office. When Frisbee passed in 2006, Dad cried like a baby.

On the day Frisbee and Tyson met, Tyson marched into the house and gave him a playful left jab to the face as he walked by. Tyson wanted to play, and Frisbee indulged him even though he was getting old and didn't have the robust energy he once had.

When it came to Dad, Tyson was as apprehensive as he was with all men. At one point, Dad walked up to Tyson as Misha was holding him and said, "Hi, Tyson!"

Tyson peered back prohibitively, to which Dad responded by challenging him to a staring contest. Dad glared into Tyson's eyes with a smirk. Tyson responded by bugging his eyes out, baring his teeth, and growling. It was hilarious. Dad laughed and said, "Look at that little dog!"

As the evening progressed, Tyson was allowed to move throughout the house and backyard freely. He and Frisbee would jump up on the screen door when they wanted to come inside, which irritated Dad because he didn't want the screen to get damaged.

"Get down!" Dad yelled at them each time.

At some point during the evening, Tyson decided he didn't like or trust Dad, because suddenly Dad yelled out, "There's a turd in my closet!"

I went to the walk-in closet he and Carla shared and sure enough, there it was: a Tyson-sized turd laid strategically on Dad's side of the closet near his shoes.

Dad wasn't pleased one bit.

"Could it be Frisbee's?" I reasoned.

"Frisbee doesn't poop in the house," Carla retorted.

We all knew the truth here. Tyson had shown his lack of pleasure with Dad by defiling his closet. Tyson was housebroken, and the only time he had "accidents" was when he was sick, if he wasn't let out in time . . . or when it was personal.

Dad had been an interior designer, and both he and Carla were very meticulous. This was a big deal to them.

Misha and I apologized emphatically, but if I'm honest, inside I was laughing my ass off. I really was sorry about Dad's closet, but he hadn't been particularly nice to Tyson. He wasn't mean to him, but he had no interest in trying to earn his trust, either. Yelling at him about the screen door had apparently pissed him off enough that he wanted to send Dad a message.

No, it wasn't right, but I respected and was entertained by his colorful expression of discontent. Subconsciously, I wondered if somehow Tyson knew about Dad's history with dogs and was getting a little revenge for Skamp and Trixie.

14: A MOMENT AT THE AHWAHNEE

Misha and I both love Yosemite National Park. Although I grew up in the San Francisco Bay Area, which is only a few hours from Yosemite, I never visited there until I was twenty. Like many people, I quickly fell in love with it. Since then, I have visited regularly—being among the majestic granite mountains always gives me a great sense of peace.

Misha grew up in Tulare County, about an hour south of Yosemite, so it has held a special place in her heart as well. That said, when we were considering venues for our wedding, Yosemite was the obvious choice. We held the wedding ceremony at the historic Yosemite Valley Chapel and the reception at the Ahwahnee Hotel.

One of the benefits of having a wedding in Yosemite was that planning it required us to make several trips there. Naturally, Tyson came along. At one point, we made a brief stop at the Ahwahnee and decided to leash Tyson to a bench just outside the main lobby entrance while we quickly went inside.

Everything seemed fine. At first. Tyson sat there obediently, apparently okay with the situation. Then we entered the hotel. In less than a minute, the piercing shriek of a tortured animal began to echo through the cavernous lobby.

Misha and I stopped in our tracks, bewildered by the sound.

"What is that?" we asked each other.

Could it be deer being hunted by ravenous coyotes? The hunting cry of some unnamed raptor? Nope. It was Tyson.

We raced back outside to investigate. *Oh, no,* I thought. *He's gonna be screaming at some unassuming park visitor or, worse yet, a park employee or ranger!*

We arrived at the bench to find him sitting there alone. No one was even paying attention to him, which was a welcome surprise. The vertical tail was wagging vigorously, his ears pinned back under duress.

"What's the deal, dude?" I asked.

"Oh, Tyson," Misha chimed in.

I picked him up and assured him that he was okay. I kissed him on the side of the face, and he licked me enthusiastically. He sure was a contradiction. A tough, independent, and confident dog. Yet at the same time, he could be so emotional, vulnerable, and needy.

Such a rich, complex soul.

"Tyson, you're such a little asshole," Misha lovingly offered as he licked my face.

"But he sure is a lover," I added.

From that point on, one of our favorite nicknames for him was "The Asshole of Love." Needless to say, I had to sit on the bench with Tyson while Misha went inside the hotel to complete our business.

15: SUPER BOBO!

For Halloween that year, I bought Tyson a Superman outfit, which seemed quite fitting. He was our little super dog, after all. The outfit, which we still have, consists of a chest plate, cape, and belt. The way the chest plate attaches causes it to barrel out, making it look like the dog has an impressive barrel chest. Tyson looked great it in, and he actually seemed to enjoy wearing it.

I agreed to meet up with Misha and her friends at Mama's, a breakfast/lunch restaurant in San Francisco's North Beach. The food there is amazing, which is one of the reasons the line to get in is always long. They don't have a waiting area; people line up on the sidewalk outside, and the staff admits customers as tables open up.

I arrived at Mama's and got in line a few minutes before Misha and her friends arrived. I couldn't help myself. I brought Tyson, in full Superman costume, with me. I hadn't thought of it as a way to meet women, but it certainly could have been if I wanted it to! Several women approached us to meet "Super Bobo!"

Misha arrived just as one of the ladies was finishing up saying hello. Misha ribbed me good-naturedly. "I better keep my eyes on you two."

As difficult as it is to believe, we never took a picture of Tyson in his Super Bobo outfit.

16: AN UNCIVILIZED TRIP TO THE MALL

We lived very close to the Stanford Mall, which is a fancy, open-air shopping center in Palo Alto, California. It has peaceful courtyards, grassy areas, fountains, and best of all, it's dog friendly. It is also near some of the wealthiest areas in the country, so the clientele can be a bit posh. Although we're anything but posh, Misha, unlike me, loves to shop—especially for clothes. She was a regular visitor to the mall.

One Saturday afternoon, she and Tyson made a trip to the mall. As they worked their way leisurely through the cornucopia of retail outlets, Tyson sniffed many plants, benches, fountains, and anything else worth sniffing. All throughout, he'd had many opportunities to relieve himself if necessary.

Eventually, they found themselves at Banana Republic, one of Misha's favorite stores. They were in there for quite a while as Misha perused the inventory and tried on numerous outfits. When she was done, she got in line to pay—when suddenly the air was engulfed by the palpable smell of doggy doo.

Misha looked down and, sure enough, Tyson had relieved himself right there in line. She looked about in horror as the fancy rich ladies around her glared at her with expressions of shock and judgment.

She quickly rushed to the front of the line and asked the clerk for a tissue with which to pick up the atrocity. The other patrons softened in light of Tyson's cuteness and Misha's obvious embarrassment. Still, where was she going to deposit it? Misha had no choice but to leave the clothes behind and find the nearest mall garbage can.

It was months before she showed her face at that store, she was so embarrassed.

Naturally, I found the incident hysterical. How could I not? Like I said before, Tyson was housebroken—but he did it anyway. This was simply a case of him not feeling like holding it in any longer.

Such a naughty little shit. The Asshole of Love, indeed.

17: SEE YOU SOON, LITTLE BUDDY

After nearly a year of planning, our wedding finally came. The festivities in Yosemite lasted a full weekend. Then, on the following Monday, we flew to Maui for a week of heaven.

Before we left, I was tasked with dropping Tyson off at the kennel, where he would stay for several days before being picked up by my Aunt Pam for the remainder of our time away.

I dreaded it. I was obviously excited about the wedding and honeymoon, but the thought of leaving Tyson with strangers for two weeks was tough. I knew he'd be okay, but he was so sensitive and emotional. I hated the idea of him being displaced and scared, even if he was a tough guy.

I walked him into the check-in area of Happiness Country Kennels in Sunol, California. Each kennel had an indoor area as well as an outdoor run which allowed for plenty of sun time and fresh air. The staff couldn't have been nicer or more welcoming. They were all women, too, which was much to Tyson's liking. They offered him dried duck and Velveeta cheese balls, which he welcomed enthusiastically. Soon, they took custody of him and assured me that he'd be fine. I was still apprehensive, but it seemed like he would be well cared for.

As I made my way to my car, I walked past the outdoor portion of Tyson's kennel. I peered over the fence at him. He looked back at me with soft, loving eyes. He seemed a little bewildered if not perfectly comfortable with the situation. I think he knew instinctively that he was in good hands. Still, I teared up a little. I hadn't been away from him for more than a day or two since he came into our lives. I was really gonna miss him!

"See you soon, little buddy," I called to him.

Our honeymoon flew by more quickly than I'd imagined. Coming back from Hawaii was a drag, but we couldn't wait to see Tyson.

It was warm out when we arrived at Aunt Pam's house to pick him up. She had the front door open with the screen door locked. I rang the doorbell and heard Tyson bark protectively as he came charging to the door, his hackles up.

"Hi, Tyson!," I said.

He quickly softened, and the vertical tail began wagging at an enthusiastic pace. Aunt Pam opened the door, and I quickly picked him up. Misha came over and we formed a circle of love, Tyson licking us excitedly.

As we talked with Pam about our trip, I continued to hold him. He buried his head in my neck affectionately, reveling in our reunion. This was something he had never done before.

Later, Misha spoke with the Happiness Country Kennels staff. They advised her that they had enjoyed Tyson so much, they didn't want him to leave.

According to the staff, he had insisted on being carried around like a baby, accompanying them on their rounds throughout the day. I wasn't surprised. What was not to love?

I was just glad he had a decent time while we were gone. It was good to be back home with my boy.

18: A TOUGH CHAPTER

A couple of months after the wedding, we bought a house in La Honda, California, which is about a half-hour drive west of Menlo Park and in a beautiful redwood forest. The house was old and in need of a lot of updating, but the location was scenic and peaceful.

Misha was thirty-five and I was thirty-three. We wanted to have a family, and we hoped children would come into the picture fairly quickly. Buying a house was an exciting first step toward this goal, as we wanted our children to have a secure childhood in one house, if possible.

Misha got pregnant right away. We were over the moon excited, as were our parents, who couldn't wait to have grandchildren. I went to work and told all of my coworkers at DHL. In the coming weeks, we slowly wrapped our brains around the idea that our little family would be growing soon.

One Friday afternoon, as I drove my delivery truck down El Camino Real in Redwood City, Misha called me on my cell phone.

"Hi, hon."

"I had a miscarriage," she cried into the phone.

"What?" I didn't want to believe what I was hearing.

"I lost the baby."

I sat there at the stoplight in complete shock. I didn't know what to say. "Are you sure?"

"Yes, I'm sure! The ultrasound showed no heartbeat!"

"Oh, honey, are you okay?"

"I've got to go."

And with that, she hung up. I just sat there, stunned. I knew there was no point in trying to call her back. There was nothing I could say that was going to make her feel better.

When I got home from work, Misha was in bed trying to sleep off the sadness. Tyson was curled up with her. I lay down with her, doing my best to comfort her. In my mind, the miscarriage was obviously an intense blow, but I had the advantage of not having a bodily connection with the baby. I had the advantage of being able to more clearly see the reality that miscarriages are quite common, and are nature's way of ensuring flawed pregnancies do not progress.

This didn't take away the loss, but it did make it easier for me to accept. Misha, on the other hand, felt not only an intense sense of loss but also that she had somehow failed the baby. She was devastated.

We spent the weekend hanging out in our little house in the woods. Even though I don't bake much, I made a homemade lasagna, which provided her with some comfort. Tyson stayed at Misha's side at all times.

Toward the end of the weekend, Misha told me Tyson was one of her greatest comforts. Before I had come home on Friday, she was lying in bed crying. Tyson had crawled into her lap, obviously trying to comfort her, and comfort her he did. She cried and cried with her head buried in his soft fur. When she was done, his coat was soaked.

It was obviously a somber moment, but it was also a special one between Misha and Tyson. Over the years, that difficult weekend has occasionally come up in conversation, and she always points out how thankful she was to have our little dog there with her. He provided her with a love and understanding that required no words, just soft, loving eyes and a desire to be there for her—a Bobo to cry on.

19: A LITTLE COMFORT FOR ME, TOO!

I had an interest in working in public safety, and La Honda had a volunteer fire department. Within a few months of buying the house, I had joined and begun the training. The hands-on wildland training happened to fall on a Saturday in the spring of 2007, not long after the miscarriage.

It was the first heatwave of the year, with temperatures reaching into the high eighties—not terribly hot, but with regular temperatures hitting highs of the mid-sixties to low-seventies, it sure *felt* hot.

Wildland firefighting is very physically rigorous, and it requires wearing a long-sleeved fire-resistant jacket, pants, a helmet, and heavy boots.

I drank plenty of water throughout the day but didn't take in enough electrolytes—a mistake I won't ever make again. Toward the end of the day, I was experiencing symptoms of heat exhaustion. Yep, I threw up. Actually, it was more like projectile vomiting. Several times.

Man, was I embarrassed. I was in fairly good shape, yet it seemed I couldn't handle a day of heavy physical work. I received a quick field medical evaluation from one of the EMTs in the group and was sent home shortly thereafter.

When I walked through the door totally exhausted, Tyson immediately knew I wasn't right. He started following me around, not wanting to leave my side. He often did this with Misha, but never with me.

I got into bed to take a nap and he insisted on joining me, which was pretty normal, as he loved to snuggle. What was strange about this instance was the *way* he snuggled with me. Usually, he'd lay on my torso or shoulder/arm and then migrate down to my legs.

This time was different. This time, he curled up on my upper shoulder, wrapping himself around the right side of my head. Usually when we cuddled, he liked to revel in the physical protection my big body provided him. This time, he seemed to be trying to comfort *me*.

He whimpered softly, letting me know he cared. I was so touched. Through the years, he was always good for a cuddle when I wasn't feeling good, but this time was particularly special. Most Tyson cuddles were mutually beneficial. Generally, this was the best you could hope for!

Most interactions with him were more about his needs than mine. That was part of his charm, though, and I benefited greatly from pouring out the love to him. It was a good feeling to have that comfort returned.

20: YOU WERE SO HOT LAST NIGHT

After the miscarriage, we were intent on "getting back on the horse" and getting pregnant as quickly as possible. The fun of making babies quickly diminished, though, when Misha didn't get pregnant. She had gotten pregnant pretty much immediately the first time, so this was bewildering. As the months passed, we kept trying, but without success.

Soon, getting pregnant began to feel like a real chore, no more pleasurable than mowing the lawn or doing the dishes. After one time in particular, I sarcastically remarked, "That was amazing, off the charts!"

"I was so turned on, I almost passed out," Misha retorted, deadpan.

The next day during a break at work, I snapped a selfie with the most ridiculous faux-seductive facial expression I could muster and sent it to Misha's phone. The caption read: "You were so hot last night."

She called me back right away and we laughed heartily at the ridiculousness of the situation. We finally agreed that we would just have to keep toughing it out until we achieved success.

Tyson snuggled with us almost every night of his life, but during our intimate moments, he was not allowed on the bed. Period. The last thing either of us wanted was to have him lying on the end of the bed and glaring at us with contempt. It would have been a real mood killer, to say the least.

So Tyson was required to hang out in his doggy bed, which was on the bedroom floor. These encounters, being more a function of necessity than pleasure, were short and to the point. Still, Tyson was not pleased. He communicated this in a very clear and consistent way.

After each encounter, I would find a fresh turd lying in the middle of the bathroom shower rug. The first couple of times, we laughed about it. After all, he *was* The Asshole of Love. He was just being his petulant little self.

But these little gifts quickly began to lose their luster, and soon I had had enough.

"Damn it, Tyson!" I yelled.

He knew he was in trouble because I rarely yelled at him. He was so sensitive that raising your voice at him really shook him up.

I stomped out of the bathroom and found him in our bedroom

doorway, looking up at me with his ears pinned back and his tail between his legs. I knew I had to do something to show him that his "presents" were not acceptable—but a spanking, even a light one, would probably traumatize him.

Instead, I grabbed him and slid him a few feet down the hallway, which had polished hardwood floors. It didn't hurt him, but the force of it definitely sent the message.

He looked up at me as if to say, "Sorry about that. Won't happen again."

And he never did do it again. He may have been The Asshole of Love, but he was no dummy.

21: HE ATE A BONE OF HIS OWN!

Misha's mom, Diane, lived on a small five-acre ranch in Tollhouse, California. We would often visit her on the weekends. She had several dogs, and Tyson would gracefully join their pack. Given how anxious he always was around new people, especially men, I was always surprised by how easily he interacted with other animals.

One of Diane's dogs was a female Great Dane-Black Lab mix named Puppy. She was enormous. When she growled, she sounded like a lion. She was so big that when she lay on the floor in front of the couch she could rest her head on the seat cushion. Despite her size, Tyson saw this as an opportunity to dominate her. By climbing onto the couch and humping her head.

It was hysterically ridiculous. Fortunately, Puppy was a gentle soul, and she would just roll with it. Maybe she saw the humor in it too.

During one of these weekend visits, everyone was outside and the dogs were all together. Soon, Tyson wandered away from the pack, and Misha lost track of him. When she found him, he was sniffing around in some bushes in an obscure, overgrown part of the yard. She called him over to her and they returned to the group.

The night we went back home to La Honda, Tyson threw up all over the bed. We weren't particularly alarmed, as he did tend to eat anything he could get his paws on. We figured maybe he ate a spider or, just as likely, something rotten.

The next day, we went to work as usual. When Misha got home, she discovered the laundry room—which was Tyson's daytime hangout—covered in blood. I worked long hours, so I didn't get home until much later.

Misha rushed Tyson to the veterinarian, where emergency surgery was performed to remove a sharp bone. Apparently, when Tyson had wandered away from the pack, he had swallowed the bone, which proceeded to tear him up inside.

Tyson stayed overnight at the vet's office. Fortunately for me, Misha was able to get home and clean up the laundry room before I had to see the carnage. The next day, he returned home all stitched up and wearing an Elizabethan collar (a.k.a. the "cone of shame").

Not long after, a friend of mine stopped by our house. During the visit, Misha had to tightly hold Tyson. Despite his frail condition, he barked and snarled protectively, fully convinced that he could take care of business. His stitches and cone of shame vibrated around as he dressed my friend down. It was so ridiculous that we all laughed, and Misha and I created a circle of love around him. He licked us happily, despite the burden of the collar.

22: IT'S PROBABLY JUST GAS!

As dog parents, the bone incident shook us up good. We were thankful Tyson had only been alone for a few hours and that we'd been able to get him help before it was too late. It made me reflect on how frail life is—how simply eating a sliver of bone could have taken our boy from us. I was thankful that emergency pet care was readily accessible and that we had the means to pay for it.

One evening a couple of months later, Tyson suddenly started oddly contorting his body. He arched his back like a cat and simultaneously made odd, airy sounds with his mouth. He didn't seem to want to eat much, either.

Misha freaked out. After the bone incident, she didn't want to take any chances, and she decided she was going to take him to the vet's office. Because it was after normal business hours, the only office available was the emergency clinic, which was very expensive.

I was a bit concerned, but it seemed to me that he probably just had gas. He was so naughty when it came to food, so who knew what he might have eaten? Misha wasn't having it, though, so off we went to emergency.

The doctor examined Tyson and said, "It's probably just gas, but I'll take an X-ray to be sure."

After the X-ray was taken, the doctor took us into the exam room and showed us the results. Even in X-ray form, Tyson's diminutive Bobo body was adorable. And, yep, you guessed it, there was a gas bubble in his stomach.

Misha and I locked eyes, and I shook my head ironically. After all was said and done, this little confirmation of gas was costing us around $300—a lot of money back in 2007 . . . and still is, actually!

The X-ray also showed that, proportionally, Tyson was quite well-endowed. We'd noticed this before, as had most everyone who met Tyson, and it had sparked more than one humorous conversation.

"He's huge, huh?" I pointed out to the doctor.

Misha laughed with a mixture of embarrassment and pride.

"Yeah, he really is," the doctor agreed.

So there it was. We had just paid $300 to confirm that Tyson had gas and a large shlong. At least we knew that he was okay.

23: ANOTHER TOUGH ONE

We continued trying to get pregnant for about a year after the miscarriage. The normal tests were performed, and it was determined that I was not, in fact, shooting blanks.

It was starting to look like we just might not be able to have children. We looked at friends who had kids with a certain sadness, but we also had faith that things would work out the way they were meant to.

Soon, there was a reason to be hopeful. Tests were also performed on Misha, and it was determined that the miscarriage had caused scar tissue in her uterus. This had likely prevented a baby from being able to attach to the uterine wall and for a pregnancy to occur. A few days later, Misha underwent a procedure to clear out the scar tissue. Within a month, she was pregnant.

Needless to say, we were excited, but it was cautious excitement. We didn't tell anyone other than our parents. Having to tell people about the miscarriage during the first pregnancy had made things much harder. We hoped and waited and carried on with life as normal as much as possible.

Around six weeks into the pregnancy, before Misha had even gone in for her first checkup, she was at a work conference in San Diego when she noticed light spotting. Although this isn't uncommon, given the miscarriage she decided to leave early and see her doctor.

An ultrasound was performed, and the baby's heartbeat was found within her fallopian tube.

This meant she had an ectopic (or tubal) pregnancy. If the pregnancy was allowed to continue, the baby would develop in the fallopian tube instead of the uterus. Eventually, the fallopian tube would rupture, and both Misha and the baby would die. The pregnancy had to be terminated.

Over the next two days, Misha had a chemically induced abortion. She had to lay in bed in significant discomfort, knowing that the baby was dying inside her body.

It was awful for both of us, but once again I had the advantage of being more objective. It was much easier for me to look at it as something that simply had to be done. I didn't have to feel it happening. I felt terrible, but all I could do was be there for her.

Once again, Tyson was her Bobo to cry on. He laid with her for two days straight, only leaving her side to eat and relieve himself. When she needed to cry, he was there to soak up her tears. When she needed love and understanding, he was there to snuggle and look at her with those soft, loving eyes that so clearly said, "I love you, Mom. I'm here for you. Things are going to be okay."

This experience was one of the toughest of Misha's life. First the miscarriage, then the long year of trying to get pregnant and not understanding why she wasn't. Then finally getting pregnant and having no choice but to take medication that would kill the baby inside of her.

I'll never fully understand the grief she felt, even though I was right there with her. Many times over the years, she has talked about how much Tyson's presence meant to her. He seemed to be able to feel on an emotional level—even a spiritual level—that she was hurting badly, and he knew exactly how to comfort her.

He was her rock, her small but mighty angel. He may have been our tough, needy little Asshole of Love, but he was there for us when it counted.

24: MICKEY MOTO NO-MO

One weekend, Misha, Tyson, and I took a trip to Napa to visit Misha's aunt and uncle, Gail and Rodger, as well as her Aunt Lynn, who was visiting from Southern California. The weather was hot, about 100 degrees, and we were all hanging out in the backyard taking occasional dips in the swimming pool.

Gail had a Chihuahua named Lola, who was an absolute sweetheart. Lola and Gail had a special bond, much like the one between me and Tyson.

That weekend, Gail and Rodger were also watching their daughter Andrea's dog, Mickey Moto. Mickey was a longhaired Chihuahua.

And he was also a total asshole.

Mickey was nasty to everyone except Andrea. He had bitten literally everyone in the family—and I do mean *everyone.*

Lots of dogs, especially Chihuahuas, are standoffish when they first meet someone. Tyson was certainly like this with most men. But Mickey Moto? He was always nasty, and he never warmed up. In fact, during most family get-togethers, Mickey had to be locked up in a separate room to keep him from biting people.

As I've said, Tyson generally got along great with other dogs, regardless of their breed. Not surprisingly, he didn't get along with Mickey.

From the moment we arrived, Mickey kept following him around. But he wasn't trying to pal around with Tyson. He was stalking him. Getting in his space and trying to intimidate him.

I thought to myself, *I wonder how long Tyson is going to put up with this?*

Within a few minutes, Tyson announced his displeasure. When Mickey tried to sneak up on his rear, Tyson spun around with his eyes bulging out of his head and his teeth bared. He growled viciously, making it clear he was ready to brawl. Mickey let out a yelp and ran into the house—not to be heard from for the rest of the afternoon.

Mickey Moto no-mo!

"Wow!" I said as we all watched the confrontation take place.

"We just watched nature take its course," Lynn observed.

I'll be the first to admit that Tyson had a habit of trying to mount every dog he shared space with. The difference was, he was also friendly with them. I had never seen him in a situation where he was being mistreated by another dog, and I was proud of how he handled himself.

He'd tried his best to get along with Mickey but realized very quickly that he was dealing with a bully. So he took action.

About a half hour later, I realized I hadn't seen Tyson for a while. I found him lying in a shady patch of clover, trying to stay cool. He lay there like a limp fish, chilling out, perfectly content.

I picked him up and said, "There's my tough guy."

He just yawned and licked my face.

25: IT'S A GIRL

Misha had been taking dressage horseback riding lessons for several years, and the inevitable had finally happened. About a month after the tubal pregnancy was terminated, Misha was thrown from her horse.

When I met her at the emergency room, her body was in a mild state of shock and she was shaking. I thought for sure she'd broken a bone or two. She was bruised up and sore, but luckily X-rays determined she didn't have any broken bones or significant injuries. We breathed a collective sigh of relief; we were scheduled to leave for Kauai, Hawaii, in a matter of days.

By the time we left for Kauai, Misha was feeling much better—still sore, but good enough to enjoy a tropical vacation. It turned out to be exactly what she needed. We had a great time just checking out of our daily routine and relaxing.

We enjoyed a Nepali Coast boat excursion, did lots of hiking and snorkeling, and enjoyed our fair share of adult beverages. Given how long it had taken us to get pregnant the second time, we really weren't too concerned about a third one happening anytime soon, so we lived life as if pregnancy were a non-issue.

The morning we returned from Kauai, Misha threw up. It seemed pretty random, as she didn't have the flu or food poisoning. Also, her period was due. It wasn't late yet, but she experienced a bit of light spotting, which was unusual for her. Just to be safe, she took a pregnancy test. Yep, you guessed it: She was pregnant!

This should have been great news, but we were still shell-shocked from the miscarriage and the ectopic pregnancy. We were also concerned that the horse accident might have hurt the baby, not to mention the fact Misha had consumed a number of alcoholic beverages in Kauai.

I was anxious about it, but Misha was practically in a panic.

She got in to see her doctor right away, and it was determined she was only a couple of weeks pregnant. The doctor was confident the baby's development was in such an early stage that neither the accident nor the alcohol would have hurt it. What a relief!

We kept our mouths shut about the pregnancy for the next ten weeks or so. We did our best not to worry about it too much. For me, this wasn't terribly difficult. After all, nothing had really changed for me. For Misha, of course, this was a whole lot harder.

Finally, at the twelve-week mark, after confirming with the doctor that the baby seemed to be developing perfectly, we revealed the good news to the world.

At the nineteen-week mark, tests for genetic and developmental abnormalities came back negative, and the sex of the baby was determined. The ultrasound technician wrote the answer on a card and sealed it in an envelope.

We went out to dinner at our favorite Chinese restaurant, Yat Sing in Redwood City, and we enjoyed a meal as we debated the sex of the baby. We had already decided on a name. If it was a girl, she would be called Madison. If it was a boy, he would be called Austin. We were both fairly sure it was a girl.

I know most men hope for a boy for their first child, but I was hoping for a girl. I wanted to feel comfortable being soft and loving with her no matter how old she got. With a boy, this would be much more difficult.

The other reason was that I actually had some concerns about being a good male role model. In retrospect, I think it was a ridiculous concern, but I've never been a stereotypical "strong male." I can put on a tough shell when needed, but I'm actually very sensitive and emotional.

There have been many times when I felt I didn't fit in well when participating in male-dominated activities like sports and firefighting, and I was worried that if I had a son he'd end up like me. I know now it was a goofy thing to worry about, but I did nonetheless.

Misha let me open the envelope from the ultrasound technician. Sure enough, the words "It's a girl!" were written on the card. We were both so pleased. The precious little package growing in Misha's tummy was a ball of love named Madison.

We couldn't wait to meet her, but we were both a bit worried about how Tyson would react. After all, he had always been our baby—our fur baby. Of course he would still be our fur baby, but there would now be a skin baby in the picture.

Tyson's world was going to change. He would have to learn to share, and we weren't sure how he was going to adjust. The only thing we knew for certain was that he would show us exactly how he felt.

We just had to hope for the best.

26: LITTLE DOGS GOT NO BALLS

While we were in Kauai, I wrote a comedy movie script, *City of Stoned*, about a small-town superhero (a ninja called The Ninya Baginya). I ended up shooting most of it while Misha was pregnant. The opening scene involves a very pregnant woman (played by Misha, of course, at around eight months along), walking toward her car while carrying a small dog (played by Tyson).

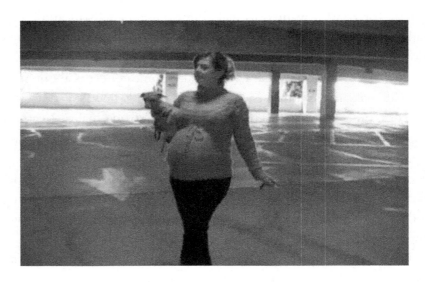

As the woman arrives at her car, a thug (played by Christopher Fuzi, who did an amazing job designing the cover of this book) attempts to mug her. Not for her money or jewelry, but for her dog!

The thug says that he hates little dogs because they "got no, you know, balls!" but his girlfriend wants one. Misha warns him that her dog is very fierce. Meanwhile, Tyson sits in her arms looking totally uncomfortable. I'm sure he probably was, what with the camera, microphone, and strange people around.

As the thug attempts to grab Tyson, Misha kicks him in the balls, gets in her car, and drives away. Then the Ninja enters and chops the thug's middle finger off in response to a vulgar gesture involving said finger.

By now I'm sure I've made it clear that Tyson really could be very fierce, but he wasn't in a fierce mood while we were shooting that scene. I probably could have gotten him all riled up by teasing him, but I wasn't going to put him through that.

Instead, I dubbed in some great audio of him barking during a game he and Misha liked to play called "Predator Momma." It involved Misha chasing him around the house and him barking fiercely as he simultaneously ran from her and postured as a tough dog.

The scene, including the sound, turned out great.

27: WELCOME, MADISON!

On April 1, 2009, I was at work driving for FedEx when I received a call from Misha. The time had come. Madison was finally about to arrive.

After being in labor at Lucille Packard Children's Hospital for most of the night, it was determined Madison was just too long to make it through the birth canal without the potential for complications. So after all that work and pain, Madison was delivered via cesarean section early on the morning of April 2.

It was a surreal experience for me. As Misha was transported to the operating room, I remember walking in a bit of a daze (I don't do well at all without sleep).

The magnitude of the situation was barely registering. My dad had told me that he didn't feel too much emotion toward me until my mom had given birth, and I was experiencing a similar process.

The operating room was filled with medical personnel, way more than I've ever seen in movies. I sat down to Misha's left and held her hand. A curtain was draped vertically at her midsection to shield us from the gore of her abdomen being cut open.

Within a few short minutes, the doctor jovially announced, "Welcome, Madison!"

Her greeting was followed by the most beautiful sound I had ever heard: the sound of Madison's first cry.

The daze I'd been in rushed out of me and was replaced by a volcanic eruption of emotion. It took all of my self-control not to burst into tears of love and joy.

A nurse placed Madison in my arms and I peered down at her, tears slowly trickling down my face.

Madison looked around, taking it all in. She seemed aware of her surroundings, as if she were entering old, familiar territory.

After I communed with Madison for a couple of minutes and Misha was done being tended by the nurses, the three of us took our first family portrait. Misha was completely exhausted. She seemed to be in the same daze I had been in a few minutes earlier.

Misha was then taken to her room so she could rest, and Madison was taken to the infant ward. I hung out with my mother-in-law, Diane, outside the ward and watched the nurse tend to Madison.

Diane was euphoric, as she finally had her first grandchild. I was also on cloud nine, so thankful that we had been blessed with the amazing experience of bringing a child into the world.

As a means of emotional defense, during the ups and downs of achieving pregnancy, I had accepted that it might not be in the cards for us.

I was now so thankful that Madison had come into our lives.

28: LET'S ALL GET ACQUAINTED

It was a relief to be back in our normal surroundings when we brought Madison home from the hospital. The question now was:

how was Tyson going to react to our new addition?

I was a bit concerned. Tyson had shown a lack of fondness for children before. On several occasions in the past when friends brought their toddlers over to visit, Tyson barked and screeched at them reproachfully when they came near him. This usually resulted in hurt feelings and tears.

Misha and I joked that we should introduce him by saying, "This is Tyson. He makes babies cry." It was yet another addition to his Asshole of Love pedigree.

The minute we walked through the door, Tyson zeroed in on Madison. The vertical tail was going enthusiastically.

Well, we thought, *this is a good sign.*

He was super curious—way more than he usually would be in a similar situation. Like most dogs, if a strange person or thing entered his space, he would check it out and either bark disapprovingly or just sniff them and walk away.

Not this time. Tyson really wanted to check Madison out. It was as if he knew that she was now part of our pack.

I sat down on the couch with Madison in my arms. Tyson jumped up and walked onto the back of the couch like a cat. Slowly, curiously, he sniffed Madison out.

He was such an adorable dog that children were always asking if they could pet him. I would always instruct them to move slowly so as not to startle him. I then kept a close watch and firm grip on him just in case.

But as Tyson examined Madison, I knew that wasn't necessary. He emoted a certain love and affection that was obvious. Soon he started to lick her lovingly.

It was a truly touching moment. He embraced Madison with his most loving self, which he only reserved for Misha and me. Unfortunately, the honeymoon wouldn't last long.

29: YOU NEED TO SEND THAT BACK

Because Madison was born via cesarean section, Misha was very sore and fragile for her first week or so home from the hospital. This meant that getting in and out of bed was a chore for her, especially since our bed was taller than most. I took a couple of weeks off from work so I could be around to help, but I wasn't available every moment. Normally, Misha being laid up in bed would have given Tyson the perfect opportunity to do what he loved most, which was to snuggle. But now there was a baby-sized obstacle named Madison.

Misha breastfed Madison, so she kept her in bed with her much of the time. This meant Tyson had to share the bed, and there were even times when he wasn't allowed on it. This was a new and very unwelcome development for The Asshole of Love, and he had no problem displaying his discontentment.

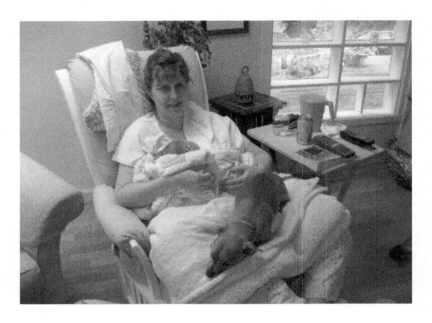

One afternoon a couple of days after bringing Madison home, I was out in the yard and Misha was in bed with the baby. Tyson had been snoozing in the living room but decided he wanted to join Misha and Madison on the bed. So he padded up to the bed, rested his front paws against it, and beckoned for Misha to lift him up.

"Sorry, Bobo," Misha said. She was in no condition to jump out of bed and carry him up. "I just can't let you up right now, but I love you."

Tyson rebuked her with his signature high-pitched screech and continued to jump up on the side of the bed. He cried out again, desperately willing her to lift him up so he could take his rightful place under the covers with her.

Misha knew how hard this had to be for him, and his palpable sadness and frustration, coupled with her own postpartum hormonal changes, made her terribly sad. She began to cry as Tyson's screeching grew angrier.

"I'm sorry, Tyson!" Misha yelled.

Apparently, Tyson wasn't convinced of her sympathy or of her inability to lift him onto the bed. So he went to Misha's dresser and looked her straight in the eyes as he lifted his leg and peed all over it. He seemed to be telepathically telling her, "I'm done playing second fiddle. You need to send that back!"

When I came in from the yard, Misha told me about the incident. I couldn't help but crack up. It was so Tyson—especially the part where he looked her in the eyes as he lifted his leg on the dresser. It was all very personal.

Honestly, I would have been surprised if he didn't act out at least a bit. Part of his charm was that he could be the sweetest dog you'd ever met, but he could also be a petulant little asshole. Just like a human being. He was our fur person, after all.

After that incident, Tyson didn't act out much. I looked out for him needing a lift onto the bed, and we both did our best to include him in everything we could. If Misha was tending to Madison, I'd make it a point to hold him or give him love. I also took him with me everywhere I could.

He really did love Madison. He just wasn't about to play second fiddle to anyone.

30: THE MOCHA AFFAIR

A couple of weeks later, we made the forty-five-minute drive to the medical clinic for Misha and Madison's checkup. Tyson came along.

Everything went smoothly. The doctor told us that Misha was recovering nicely and Madison was as healthy as she could be. But on the drive back, about five minutes away from home, Misha suddenly freaked out. There was a strange fleshy substance oozing from the stitches of her cesarean incision. The only thing we could do was turn around and head back to the doctor's office.

Forty minutes later, we arrived. As it turned out, the oozy substance was a discharge of fatty tissue, which we learned was common with cesareans. The doctor wrote Misha a prescription for antibiotics and we headed to the CVS pharmacy at the Sharon Park shopping center in Menlo Park.

By now we were both famished, and I was starting to feel a little light-headed, so I bought Misha and myself a couple of coffees and cookies. With Misha and Madison in the back seat, I gave her the cookies and her drink and put mine in the car cup holder. Then I went to the pharmacy to pick up the prescription.

When I finally got back, I climbed into the car and eagerly reached for my mocha. I knew a little sugar and caffeine would make me feel much better. To my horror, I discovered Tyson had chewed the cap off the cup, lifted the cup out of the holder, and dumped the contents onto the front passenger seat. He was now delightedly lapping up my precious mocha off the seat.

"God damn it, Tyson!" I yelled.

He didn't even look up at me. He just kept on lapping.

I was furious. Not only did I not have my mocha, but now I was going to have to have the seat shampooed if I didn't want my car to reek of rotten milk.

"You little shit!" I shouted, then grabbed him and tossed him into the back seat.

I was mad at Tyson, but I was also mad at myself. He was always trying to steal any food he could get his paws on. I should have known he'd go for the mocha.

Misha handed me a cookie and said, "Let's just get home."

The Sharon Park parking lot was notorious for bad drivers, and it was packed. Since we were in a diagonal space at the end of one of the aisles, I figured the best way to exit quickly was to back out of the aisle and onto the intersecting entryway.

As I did this, a lady in a yellow Mercedes came down the aisle. My maneuver forced her to stop so I could back out of her way. She didn't like being held up. She honked her horn and flailed her hands, mouthing expletives.

The irony was that once I was out of her way, the aisle was still too backed up to even move forward. This meant her tantrum was utterly pointless.

There she sat, still, right in front of me with my car about twenty yards to her right. I was already cranky and mad at Tyson, but now I was seriously pissed. I knew what I had to do.

Before I could change my mind about it, I floored it. My car was a Jeep Cherokee, and it had a fair amount of starting power. The car lunged forward, the engine racing as I headed straight at the woman and her yellow Mercedes.

I cut the wheel to the left and stopped about ten yards from her. I hadn't been going terribly fast, but it scared the pants off of her nonetheless! The woman practically jumped out of her seat as she mouthed the words, "Oh, shit!"

It was immensely satisfying. I just pointed at her, threw my head back, and laughed as emphatically as I could. Then I slowly drove away.

Misha was tending to Madison, so she had no idea why I'd done what I had done. At first, when I told her, she was a bit shocked, but her shock quickly turned to laughter. Like I said, that parking lot was notorious, and she'd had her own fair share of run-ins with bad, angry drivers.

We laughed our asses off. Not just at the Mercedes run-in, but also at all the other events of the afternoon. The laughter was exactly what we needed.

31: A CONSTANT COMPANION

Misha was lucky enough to be able to stay home from work with Madison for the first four months of her life. I was laid off by DHL when they downsized their domestic workforce, and although I was working two part-time jobs at FedEx and California State Parks, I had more time off than normal.

This extra time together as a family was precious, and Tyson was right there in the middle of it, embracing his role as Madison's brother.

When Misha returned to work, her dad, Mike, stayed with us for eight months until Madison was a year old. It was generous of him, as he lived (and still lives) in San Diego, so he had to fly back and forth quite a bit. For us, it was a blessing to have a trusted family member watching over Madison while we were working, especially when she was so young.

Every day, Mike would take her for walks through the forested roads of La Honda with Tyson always there by their sides. Then Mike would take them to have lunch with Misha in Menlo Park.

Through it all, Tyson took full advantage of his brotherly position, especially when Madison was eating. He loved to hover around her high chair as she was enjoying Cheerios or macaroni and cheese, eagerly waiting for her to drop food on the floor. He scored so much food that he started to gain weight. By the time we realized the impact his scavenging was having, Tyson had put on three pounds—a heck of a lot, considering his normal weight was eight pounds. Now he was tipping the scale at a staggering eleven pounds!

In November of 2009, when Madison was seven months old, I was accepted into the California State Parks ranger academy. This included a six-month stint at the police academy at the old Fort Ord Army base, plus two months at a park operations academy on the conference grounds of Asilomar State Beach. Both were near Monterey, California, and were beautiful locations, but they were also a four-hour round trip from La Honda. This meant I had to be away from home during weekdays for eight months. I knew it would be tough.

The night Misha and Madison dropped me off, the weight of the next eight months seemed overwhelming. I looked at Madison in her baby seat and cried like a baby.

Still, I had it better than many. Half of my classmates were from Southern California and didn't have the luxury of visiting with their families every weekend.

Once I got settled in and focused on the demands of the academy, things got easier, but I was still homesick. Each night, I called home to check on everyone. Some nights were more chaotic than others, and I knew Misha had her hands full.

"How are things?" I asked one night. "How is Madison?"

"Busy!" Misha replied, not an ounce of humor in her voice.

I was busy too, but I'd be lying if I said I didn't feel a certain level of guilt over Misha having to run the household without me to pitch in.

Tyson's constant companionship helped us both a lot. He was always there by Misha's side, helping to maintain a sense of love and normalcy that gave her peace. Sure, he was his demanding, emotional self, but he gave what he took. Each night when Misha settled in with the day's many tasks completed, he was there to cuddle and snuggle.

"How's the Bobo?" I asked.

"He's right here," she replied with love and peace in her voice.

"Can you put the phone near him so I can say hi?"

"Okay, go ahead."

"Hi, Tyson!" I said. "I miss you, buddy."

Misha told me that every time I did that, Tyson's ears would perk up and he'd lick the phone. It gave me peace to know that he was taking good care of Misha.

32: SIR HUMPS-A-LOT

Mom came to visit for Madison's first birthday and brought her dogs, Comet and Rudy. They stayed with us for a few days. The dogs got along fine, and Tyson did his standard share of humping.

The photo of Madison shown here, which was taken by Mom, displays Tyson's wholly inappropriate actions, in addition to his uncanny photo bomb abilities.

Rudy looks on in resignation as Tyson goes to town on Comet.

33: THANKS FOR WAITING UP, PAL

Upon completing the academy and field training, my reporting location was the state beach at Half Moon Bay, a coastal town about a half hour south of San Francisco.

This was the same park where I had worked as a part-time park aide before my acceptance into the ranger academy. I was lucky to be able to return here, as I could have been assigned to many places throughout the state. The beaches and coastal forests in and around Half Moon Bay are incredible, and I had the opportunity to work with a number of rangers and lifeguards who had mentored me before. I was blessed with wonderful colleagues in a fantastic location.

As great a job being a law enforcement officer in the parks is, it has its stressful moments. Most enforcement contacts are cordial, many even friendly, but some are very confrontational and stressful. I knew this was the reality of the job, and I embraced it willingly—but it still took some getting used to.

After I completed a contact, I always self-critiqued my performance—every aspect, including my social skills, and if my decision to write or not write a citation, or make an arrest, had been appropriate. Things got easier over time, but in the beginning it was tough, especially when a contact was particularly confrontational. I always tried to figure out ways I could have helped the interaction be more positive. Sometimes it was obvious there was nothing I could have done. Other times, it wasn't so clear and I'd beat myself up.

Being the new guy, I worked the swing shift. I'd go on duty in the late morning to early afternoon, and I wouldn't get off duty until the late evening. This meant I often woke after Misha and Madison had left for work and school, and I didn't get home until after they were already asleep. Even though we were all in the same home, it often felt lonely.

Thankfully, Tyson was always waiting for me to come home at night, and he'd be there to hang out with me in the morning. When I came home, Misha would be in bed fast asleep, but he'd be on my side of the bed outside the covers. I was touched. I knew he loved to be burrowed under the covers with Misha, but he also felt a duty to watch over her, and Madison too, until I came home.

"Thanks for waiting up for me, pal," I'd whisper.

I'd heat up my dinner in the microwave, and he'd insist on sitting by my side and begging for a nibble here and there. After those particularly grueling shifts, it was always a comfort to be able to pick him up and love on him and let him lick me to death. Even when a member of the public seemed to hate my very soul, Tyson was always there to soothe me and show me I was still worthy of his love. This always made things a little easier.

As soon as I finished eating, he'd walk to the hallway and let me know he wanted to go back to bed. When I finally came to bed, Tyson would be under the covers, burrowed in with Misha, his nightly protective duties complete.

34: IT'S THE SHIH TZU!

Upon my completion of the academy, we moved to San Carlos, which is a beautiful suburb in San Mateo County. We lived on a nice street lined with duplexes, many of which were home to other dogs. One of these dogs was a Shih Tzu that, for some reason, Tyson didn't like.

Misha had told me several stories about encountering the Shih Tzu while on a walk with Tyson, and that he always reacted to the poor guy with venom—snarling, barking, and trying to nip. Misha always kept a tight hold on Tyson, but apparently the dog's owners weren't too friendly. Misha described them as snooty.

Our front door faced the street, about twenty-five yards from the sidewalk, and there was no screen door. One warm day, we were sitting in the living room with the front door open.

Madison was in the midst of scolding us for telling her she couldn't have a cookie.

"You! You no say no to me!" she lectured, her antenna-like ponytail bouncing with attitude.

"All this over a cookie?" Misha asked.

"Cooookiiie," Madison whined.

Just as I began to imitate her mockingly, Tyson bolted out the door toward the street, barking viciously. Misha ran after him, and within a few seconds, I heard her scream.

"Brandon! It's the Shih Tzu!!!"

I took off out the door, screaming for Tyson to come back. The poor Shih Tzu and his mom were frozen at the end of the driveway as Misha tried unsuccessfully to grab Tyson, who read the "intruders" the riot act.

Apparently, there was something about my presence that made Tyson a little more mellow. He probably saw me as the protector and didn't feel as vulnerable when I was around. When I took him to the veterinarian, for example, he was generally mellow and cooperative. When Misha took him, they usually had to muzzle him.

Fortunately, this proved true in the case of the Shih Tzu. I quickly scooped Tyson up and apologized to both victim and owner. The Shih Tzu seemed like a sweet little guy, and his owner didn't seem too bad, either. I guessed Tyson had been much more aggressive in their previous encounters.

"Oh, Tyson," Misha lamented after we brought him back inside.

"Bobo! You're a crazy-ass dog!" I added.

He just licked my face like nothing had happened. With the attack thwarted, Madison finally got her cooookiiie. I believe it was oatmeal raisin.

35: OUR LITTLE SAVIOR

In March of 2011, Misha and I went to Arizona for professional baseball spring training. Misha's mom, Diane (now known to

Madison as "Gogo") came to San Carlos to take care of Madison and Tyson while we were away.

One morning at around 2 a.m., Diane called Misha in a near panic. They had all been asleep when Tyson started coughing loudly. Diane and Madison awoke to a room filled with smoke. A small electrical fire had started in the kitchen and had thankfully gone out on its own.

Misha instructed Diane to call 911, which she did. When the fire department came, they discovered some faulty wiring and disconnected electricity to the area. They advised that the fire could have restarted at any time, so it was very fortunate she woke up and called when she did.

We couldn't help but wonder if carbon monoxide from the smoke, or even a more serious fire, might have been fatal if Tyson hadn't been there.

Our little savior had protected the family.

36: NO MORE HIP

Not long after the fire, Tyson's limp became more pronounced. It was clear that the pain in his hip was getting significantly worse. We decided it was time to have his hip removed. He was now seven years old, and we had been putting off the surgery for six years.

I dropped him off at the veterinarian in the morning and picked him up the following afternoon. He was still drugged up, and to add insult to injury he was wearing the cone of shame. He looked absolutely miserable. I felt terrible for him.

The good news was he didn't take long to bounce back and start behaving like his normal self. He still had a tendency to hold his right rear leg up when he walked, but he didn't seem to be hurting.

I'd always remind him, "Use your leg, Bobo. We paid a lot for that!"

That propensity to hold his leg up stayed with him for the rest of his life. I'm not sure why. Maybe the cartilage that grew back in his hip's place didn't feel stable enough, or maybe the action became so habitual that it felt more comfortable.

The surgery was expensive, which was why we waited so long to get it done, but I'll always regret not taking care of it sooner. The pain seemed to be pretty tolerable, right up until it clearly wasn't.

Animals don't show their pain like humans do, and unfortunately, they can't express it in words. I now know that the pain had been pretty bad for a while; much worse than one could tell—but I'll explain more about that in a later chapter.

37: NUMBER 27

Misha and I both believed each of us had an extraordinarily strong soul connection with Tyson. We knew instinctively that he had come into our lives for a reason.

Most dog owners I know consider their dogs to be a valued part of the family. The same goes for most cat owners I know. But Tyson wasn't just a member of our family. He was our shared soul mate.

He had opened my heart and facilitated a healing I can only describe as "meant to be."

For Misha, he provided a lot of joy, comfort, and companionship. She adored him. Because of this, the experience she had during his next trip to the kennel wasn't terribly surprising.

In October of 2011, we went to Maui and left Tyson with a kennel in San Carlos. Hawaii was and is one of our favorite places in the world to visit, but we always missed Tyson a lot while we were gone. Coming home was always a letdown, but our desire to get back to him always made things easier.

Our plane arrived back in San Francisco on a Sunday evening around eight o'clock. We were exhausted from the flight and went straight to bed. We both had to work the next day, so Misha planned on picking Tyson up at the kennel after work.

The next morning, Misha told me she had a horrible nightmare about Tyson. In the dream, they were on opposite ends of a dark, foggy field, and they were desperately trying to get to each other. No matter how hard she tried to run to him, her body only moved in slow motion, like she was in a viscous fluid. Tyson yelped at her sadly, but she was helpless to get to him.

I interpreted the dream as just indicating she had missed him a lot, but Misha was very emotionally affected by it. Sometime later that morning, she called me and announced, "I'm going to get him on my lunch break. I'm worried about him."

"Okay," I said, "will you have enough time?"

"If I'm late, I'm late. Something isn't right."

"Well, give him a hug for me."

When she called me later, Misha told me how relieved she was to have picked Tyson up early. Then she swore she'd never use that kennel again. The lady working the reception desk had been cold and aloof when Misha arrived, and had called back to another staff member and said, "Can you get Number 27?"

Misha was taken aback. After all, Tyson was not just a number—and a business devoted to the care of pets shouldn't be referring to their guests by their kennel number. When they brought him out, Tyson went ballistic. He was so excited to be leaving that he practically came out of his skin, kissing Misha and convulsing with excitement.

This reaction was in stark contrast to his behavior during past pickups at Aunt Pam's or the other kennels we had used. Those times, he had certainly been happy to see us, but not like this. His level of excitement seemed to indicate he was way too relieved to be getting out of there.

I asked Misha how he was doing now, and she said that he was great, back to his normal self. She brought Tyson back to work with her and had to hide him under her desk—a hard task, considering he snarled every time a strange man came around. Yep, back to his normal self.

"You see?" Misha said. "I knew something was wrong."

"Yeah, he must have been reaching out to you."

"I think so."

Soul mates indeed.

38: I HAVE A FLEA!

Another incident where Tyson telepathically communicated with Misha occurred sometime in 2012. I was at work. Misha was home with Madison and Tyson and was getting ready to go grocery shopping.

Thwarting her efforts to get out the door was Madison, who was in full toddler mode and getting into everything. Misha had just returned all of the scattered plastic bowls to the kitchen cupboard when she heard Madison rummaging through a drawer in her room.

"Madison, we have to go!" she called, hoping there wasn't yet another mess waiting for her to clean up. She stomped quickly down the hall into Madison's room, hoping to mitigate any potential disaster—and when she got there, sure enough, Madison was rummaging through her previously folded clothes.

But what jumped out at Misha was the way Tyson was seated in the doorway, staring up at her forlornly.

"What's wrong, Bobo?" Misha asked.

Tyson answered by turning his head in the direction of his left rear flank. Misha couldn't explain how, but she knew intuitively that Tyson was telling her he had a flea.

She knelt down and searched his body. Sure enough, she found one flea exactly where Tyson had gestured. She searched the rest of his body, but fortunately, there were no more. She sure could read him!

39: A NEW HOME, A NEW PUP

By the fall of 2013, we had saved up enough money for a down payment on a home. Unfortunately, homes in San Mateo County and anywhere on the San Francisco Bay Area peninsula were out of our price range due to the high-tech and biotech boom. We ended up finding a great home in Castro Valley across the Bay. Not only did I grow up there, but the schools were great and the homes were relatively affordable (at least compared to the peninsula). The buying process was completed in December, and we finally moved in just before Christmas.

I had been wanting to adopt another dog for some time, but Misha didn't think it would be a good idea until we had a home of our own with enough room to accommodate two dogs. Her concern was valid, but I wanted to offer a shelter dog a home as soon as possible. Now we had our own home with plenty of room for a second dog!

I hadn't been in an animal shelter for years, and definitely not since Tyson had reopened my heart. When I walked into the Hayward Animal Shelter and told them I was interested in adopting a dog, and that I was hoping for a Chihuahua, they said that I was in luck—almost all of the dogs available were either Chihuahuas or pit bulls. I found this to be pretty sad. A lot of the dogs at the shelter were strays from the Hayward area. That meant that, for whatever reason, people in the area tended to abandon Chihuahuas and pit bulls.

I was shown into the viewing area and soon found myself surrounded by the hopeful faces of the many dogs and cats needing a home. I felt a burst of sadness that almost brought me to tears, but I got hold of myself as one stubborn tear fought its way onto my face. I reminded myself that I was there to give one of these beautiful creatures a home. But I wanted them all to have a home.

I stopped and visited with each of the dogs, regardless of whether they were a candidate for adoption. I narrowed my selection down to three Chihuahuas. I was given an opportunity to visit with each of them in a separate room, and I tried to keep in mind that I needed to be realistic about which dog would be the best fit, regardless of how much I wanted to help them.

When the second dog, a Chihuahua/Jack Russell mix named Chloe, was brought into the room, it was obvious she was the one. She was friendly, energetic, and she didn't seem skittish at all. She was also very cute. I knew instinctively that she would be a good fit.

The next day, Misha, Madison, Diane (who was visiting), and Tyson came to the shelter with me to meet Chloe. Madison fell in love with her right away, and Misha thought she was great too. Chloe was taken into a private room to meet Tyson, and they got along fine. Soon, Chloe arrived at her new home.

Tyson seemed to be fine sharing his space with Chloe. To be fair, he didn't seem to care one way or the other. By now he was very secure with his place in our lives, and he wasn't concerned about a newcomer edging him out. However . . . he tried to mount Chloe a couple of times to establish dominance.

Chloe wasn't pleased. At all. She growled and barked at Tyson fiercely until he simply slinked away, apparently unaffected by her threats. It was as if he were saying, "Fine, have it your way. We both know I rule this roost."

Chloe, being a few pounds heavier and lacking the burden of a bad hip, was physically stronger than Tyson. She had also roamed the streets of Hayward for an undetermined length of time and had already had a litter of puppies, according to the veterinarian.

When it came to food, she had to be fed first. Otherwise, she would try to eat Tyson's, as well. We figured she probably had to claw for every meal she had eaten on the streets, so it was a survival instinct.

In every other way, though, Tyson was the alpha in their relationship. Chloe would follow him around, often sleeping in his bed with him.

If Tyson was in his kennel, she would snuggle up with him. Sometimes he would grunt at her irritably, but mostly he just rolled with her presence.

Their relationship was something like that of an older brother and a kid sister—a salty teenage boy with a baby sister who always insisted on tagging along.

I'm sure some of this had to do with the fact she was the newcomer in a world where Tyson was adored, but mostly I believe it was their nature.

Tyson wanted things his way, and he was perfectly comfortable making sure everyone knew it. Chloe just wanted to be in a secure home where she was loved.

Even today, with Tyson gone, she still carries the same disposition. If he came back as a puppy right now, he'd still be the alpha in their relationship.

He would also appreciate her more. I know this because of information I received after he passed on.

But more on that later . . .

40: ANT TRAPS! DELICIOUS!

That first summer in the new house, we had a bit of an ant problem. To combat this, we put ant traps in various locations around the house. For those who don't know how these traps work, the trap is loaded with poisonous bait, and ants are attracted to its odor. The ants take the poisonous bait back to their nest, killing the queen.

The problem was that Tyson was also drawn to the odor. He even chewed up one of the traps. In retrospect, I don't know why we were surprised. That dog wanted to eat everything!

The problem was we couldn't determine how much poison he'd consumed. So the veterinarian had to pump his stomach and keep him overnight for observation.

I'll be the first to admit I probably contributed to his food obsession. After all, one of the ways I bonded with him was by giving him small nibbles of food from my plate. I continued to do this for the rest of his life.

That said, Tyson knew very well what the boundaries were. He knew he was only allowed to eat people food if it was given to him. He also knew he would get in trouble and be denied any further treats if he took food without permission.

We always had to keep an eye on him when food was around, but he was generally pretty good about being patient and waiting for nibbles to be given to him. That was, until now.

He was about ten years old at this point, and apparently, he had decided the rules were for other dogs. Like Chloe. She, too, had always enjoyed little nibbles, but even to this day, she respects the boundaries.

Not long after the ant trap incident, we all enjoyed a little fun at Tyson's expense. We were having pizza for dinner, and as we often do, we were eating around the coffee table in the living room.

When I looked up at the television and away from my plate, Tyson boldly grabbed a slice of pizza right off my plate. I saw him make his move from the corner of my eye and snatched it out of his mouth, but not until he had devoured half of it.

It was amazing how quickly such a little dog could eat, especially when he knew he wasn't supposed to.

Misha just shook her head and said, "That dog!"

Madison yelled, "You bad dog, Tyson!"

"Damn it, Tyson!" I threw in. "Why? Why?! You know I'll share with you!"

Adjacent to the coffee table was an open sliding glass door leading out to our back patio. I picked Tyson up, put him outside, and slid the door closed.

We all returned to our meal as he gazed in with the most pathetic, forlorn face I'd ever seen. It was extremely satisfying!

I made a big production out of every bite I took, saying things like, "You sure are missing out, Tyson!" or "Tyson, doesn't this look good?!"

He was beside himself. He yelped and screamed in anger and disbelief. He especially hated it when I called Chloe over for a bite. It was hysterical, and we all enjoyed the show.

Finally, after the entirety of the meal, I opened the door for him. As he ran inside, he gave me one last disgruntled bark. I wish I could say this brief lesson changed his behavior, but I'd be lying if I did.

He certainly learned the lesson. He knew it all too well! But like everything, Tyson did things *his* way, and there would be many more food lessons to come.

41: THE ESCAPE ARTIST

Whenever we left the dogs home alone, they stayed in the garage. This was for a couple of reasons. First, Chloe often peed in the house if no one was around to let her out—and Tyson had a penchant for peeing in the house if he had grievances . . . such as the fact we weren't home with him. Second, the house was a tri-level with no air conditioning, and the garage was one of the coolest places.

No dog wants to be locked up all day, and we certainly didn't take any pleasure in having to confine them. However, the backyard wasn't safe for them, as our house backed up to a wilderness area with coyotes, mountain lions, and all sorts of other wild creatures. Thus, the garage was about the best we could do for them.

As you might imagine, it didn't take long for Tyson to find a way to escape. The garage had an air vent near the ground on the wall closest to the driveway. Even though we had storage boxes that we thought blocked enough of the vent to keep the dogs from escaping, you know what they say: Where there's a will, there's a way.

Tyson clawed and chewed at the drywall along the edge of the vent to create enough room for his tiny body to squeeze through—and since the grating on the outside of the vent was loose on one side, he was able to slither out.

One day I got home and opened the door leading from the living room to the garage. Chloe ran into the house, but not Tyson. I called out for him, thinking maybe he was sleeping in a corner or something, but there was no response, not even the sound of his collar shaking around. I inspected the garage, discovered the escape passage, and realized he was gone.

I have to admit I panicked, even though we lived on a cul-de-sac with very little traffic. I was hopeful he hadn't gone too far and was safe. Still, I would have been devastated if anything happened to him.

I raced out to the front of the house, and there he was. Moseying down the sidewalk like he had business there.

"Bobo! You crazy-ass dog!" I scolded.

He walked up to me with those soft, loving eyes and his vertical tail wagging steadily, happy to see me. Not excited, mind you. Just pleased.

"What am I gonna do with you, Tyson?"

I picked him up and kissed him on the side of the face, relieved he was okay. I was also very thankful I didn't have to worry for long, and that I'd found him right away.

I used wood and bricks to block the outside of the vent, and I arranged the boxes more strategically to prevent Tyson from attempting any future escapes. He never got out again, but I know he tried because more of the wall was chewed up in the coming weeks.

Later, I spoke with a neighbor who had seen Tyson when he got out. She laughed and told me Tyson just sat on the front porch, barking at anyone and anything that passed by. He hadn't wanted to explore, thank goodness—just spend the day on his own terms.

42: A COMFORT DURING A DIFFICULT TIME

A few months after we moved to Castro Valley, I decided to apply for a job with a park police department very close to our new home. I loved being a Ranger with California State Parks, but my commute to Half Moon Bay was a minimum of forty-five minutes without traffic. This alone made it a no-brainer. There was also the fact that the new job would pay about fifty percent more, and the jobs were similar. It would have been hard to justify not trying, at least, so I did. I was hired, and I started in August of 2014.

Transitioning to a new police department is a challenging process, regardless of how long you've been doing it. Every department has its own culture and different ways of accomplishing the same tasks. This is also the case among departments tasked with patrolling parklands.

Part of the challenge is navigating the field training process, in which the new-hire is paired with several different Field Training Officers to be shown the department's procedures, as well as to be evaluated with regard to their ability to perform their duties safely and competently. Ultimately, the new-hire will either successfully navigate the process or they'll be terminated from employment.

What made the process difficult for me was that I'd given up a secure job to make the move to the new department. If things didn't work out, I could go back to my old job but the hiring process would take at least a year. Absurd, yes, but it is the State of California, after all!

A year without a steady income would have been catastrophic with our new mortgage. It was a mentally difficult process, but one I had to battle through.

I had my ups and downs, as expected, and although I missed State Parks, I never doubted my decision to make the move—at least while I went through the field training program.

I was signed off as a solo officer in January of 2015 and assigned to the graveyard shift: nine p.m. to seven a.m.

I've never been much of a night person. At overnight birthday parties, I was always the first one to fall asleep. I stayed up all night a few times in college, as well as a few times for work when I worked in film and television, but always out of necessity and never by choice. Now it was going to be a way of life.

I hated sleeping all day and being up all night. For one, I just didn't sleep as well, and therefore didn't feel great during the night. But more importantly, it put me on the opposite schedule as that of my family. I felt disconnected from them, even though I still saw them every night before leaving for work.

All that said, the worst part of this shift was my sergeant, my immediate supervisor. He was one of those guys who desperately needed to play the role of the stereotypical macho cop. When I say macho, I don't mean tough. You have to have a certain amount of toughness to be a police officer, and I consider that a positive trait. This guy, though, was a real hard-ass, and insensitive.

He was the kind of cop who makes you feel like he couldn't give a shit less about you. The kind of cop you hope doesn't pull you over because no matter how minor your offense, he's gonna treat you like Public Enemy Number 1. The kind who gets a rush out of portraying the hard-boiled cop, regardless of how benign the situation might be.

To be clear, I think most police officers are great people with a very high level of integrity. Most of them want to help people. The hard-boiled stereotype isn't as common as many people assume. Even my sergeant, I believe, wanted to help people.

True to form, this sergeant loved to be particularly hard on lateral officers (those who came from other law enforcement agencies). After all, he had to show new-hires just how bad-ass he and his department were! He had even put a thirty-year veteran and former Special Response Unit sergeant through the wringer. I would be no different.

From the start, I could do no right. If I wrote a citation, he'd say I should have cited another code, even though this was totally at my discretion.

If I chose not to write a citation out of the interest of justice, he'd say I had made a bad decision. If I rightly determined that physical force was not necessary to be used on a cooperative suspect, he'd criticize me.

He didn't view his officers as colleagues he was there to lead and support. He viewed us as problems to be fixed. The issue was that his definition of a "problem officer" was one who didn't do things precisely as he did.

My nature is to see the best in people. I didn't see the sergeant as a bad person. I just figured we needed to get to know and trust one another.

Each night, I did my best to make decisions based on what I thought he wanted. But no matter what I did, no matter how sure I was that he'd be pleased, he found some reason to criticize me.

My stress level during this time was nearly through the roof. Not only was my body out of whack, but I felt like a total failure almost every day.

At State Parks, I was liked and respected; I believed I was an effective peace officer. It now seemed I had been kidding myself. I began to think that maybe I had made a big mistake coming to the new department.

To make matters worse, my employment was still probationary. My sergeant's evaluation of me would undoubtedly play an important role in determining if I would complete my probation. Not only was I miserable, but there was a chance I could lose my job.

Each morning when I'd come home from work, I'd eat a quick snack and go to bed. Tyson, who had been asleep all night, was more than happy to join me. If I didn't mention it already, he was about the laziest dog you'll ever meet.

He'd crawl under the covers and snuggle up with me, giving me a constant comfort that really helped.

The future might have been uncertain, my confidence may have been shot, and I might have felt alone and separated from my family, but my boy was there.

He was there to stand on my chest and lick my face as he always did before retiring under the covers. With his silky soft fur, Tyson was there to snuggle and provide companionship; companionship that was a reminder to me in those lonely days that I was loved, and that everything would be okay.

My time with this sergeant came to a merciful end a few months later. His evaluation of me was awful, but fortunately, his superiors disagreed. I've gone on to enjoy a successful and enjoyable career, and I hope to continue to do so for many years to come.

I'll always remember this time as one of the more difficult of my life, but I'm so thankful that my Bobo was there to make things just a little easier.

43: I'M NOT WALKING ANOTHER STEP

Our home in Castro Valley was only a few minutes' drive to Lake Chabot, a regional park with a beautiful lake and great trails for hiking and biking.

Around the same time I started working for the new department, Misha took Tyson, Chloe, and Madison for a walk along the lake.

They had been hanging out at home all day, and a cranky Madison was driving Misha nuts. She was only five years old, so it was destined to be a fairly short hike, but they all needed to get out of the house.

As I've said before, Tyson may have been full of personality but he was also incredibly lazy. Even when he was young, sleeping was one of his favorite activities.

He enjoyed walks, but they were generally pretty short. Part of this was because of his bum leg, but an equal amount was due to him simply being lazy. He definitely didn't need a large yard—or any yard, really—to romp around in. He had been a great apartment dog.

From the start, the walk was more trouble than it was worth. Madison's crankiness continued, and she complained relentlessly.

Chloe, always energetic, was happy as a clam, but Tyson started to protest all forward motion after about a half mile. At first, he kept stopping, then reluctantly inching forward. Pretty soon, he refused to walk any farther.

"Okay," Misha announced, "we're turning back."

"Good!" Madison said. "I hate this walk!"

"You need to improve your attitude, Madison."

"Can I get a hot chocolate at the marina?"

"If you can walk all the way back without complaining, yes!"

"Okay, Mommy."

For Madison, the promise of hot chocolate was all the motivation she needed to continue without protest. Tyson was a different story. As they began the return walk, Tyson took a few steps then stopped again.

"Come on, Bobo. We have to walk back," Misha coaxed, but he looked up at her as if to say, "I'm not walking another step."

She tugged at his leash, but instead of walking Tyson lay down on the pavement. She tugged some more, but he just allowed himself to be dragged along as he gazed obstinately into her eyes. Flabbergasted, she tugged again with the same result.

"Are you kidding me, Tyson?" she scolded.

No, he definitely wasn't kidding. Misha wound up having to carry him all the way back to the car.

She called me on the phone to tell me about their adventures. I knew it would be another ridiculous Tyson story when she started with, "That dog!"

I giggled as I learned of her day of captivity with "our kids."

In the end, all I could say was, "The Asshole of Love. He really is one of a kind."

TYSON'S GIFT

What follows are photos of lazy Tyson in various states of repose.

44: THE GINGERBREAD BANDIT

Since our move to Castro Valley, Tyson's food violations had become more and more frequent. The previously mentioned pizza incident was just one example. Besides being more brazen about trying to take food from our plates, he had also become far more adept at stealing food from backpacks, containers, and other things.

We could always tell when Tyson had been up to no good because his right front shoulder would get sore, and he'd hold that paw up to avoid putting weight on it. His bad rear hip had caused him to compensate by putting extra weight on his right front shoulder, and over time Tyson developed arthritis there.

Tyson was right-pawed, which meant he used his right paw to commit nefarious acts like breaking into my backpack to steal protein bars (he would accomplish this by tearing the zipper open; not unzipping it, but separating the teeth). We called it his "probing paw."

At first, we didn't see the correlation between the sore "probing paw" and the food violations. We assumed Chloe, being more physically capable, must have been the culprit. After it happened several more times, though, Misha began to insist it was Tyson.

I was skeptical, but she presented the compelling evidence that every time it happened we would find him under the dining room table (his "lair," as Misha called it) with the torn-open protein bar wrappers. Also, after each incident, he would look like an engorged tick in comparison to Chloe, who looked normal. She might have enjoyed some of his take on occasion, but it became quite clear that Tyson was our food burglar.

Even though I continued to share small nibbles of food with him, his begging became more and more aggressive. If I didn't share with him quickly enough, he'd do what we affectionately called "excitasneeze" (pronounced excite-a-sneeze) where he'd sneeze over and over and over to show how much he wanted a treat. If that didn't work, he'd start yelping at me.

It didn't change anything; I'd actually give him less. Still, he persisted. He was also far more forceful about begging from Misha while she was cooking. He loved vegetables, especially carrots, and if Misha was preparing a salad, he'd yelp at her and jump up on her legs until she gave him one.

"Get out of here, Tyson, you little rodent!" she'd scold.

This brings me to a particularly memorable food burglary—one of Yuletide proportions. In December of 2016, we hosted a Christmas party at our home. Since there would be a fair number of children in attendance, Misha bought a bunch of gingerbread house kits. The kits included gumdrops, cinnamon hard candy, frosting, and, of course, the gingerbread walls and roof.

The party was a success, and the kids enjoyed making the gingerbread houses, but there were three kits left over. Given that the kits came packaged in sealed plastic bags inside of cardboard boxes, Misha figured they'd be safe to store in one of the kitchen cupboards for use the following Christmas. Given Tyson's propensity for going after sealed protein bars, we should have known better.

Fast-forward a few months later, after we'd forgotten all about the gingerbread house kits. Misha came home after leaving Chloe and Tyson alone in the house for a couple of hours. She'd left the back door open for them so they could go outside if they needed to, so she thought things would be okay. She was wrong.

When Misha walked through the front door, Chloe guiltily got up from her bed and slinked away, out of sight. Tyson did not move. He only stared up at Misha with an innocent expression. Misha knew something wasn't right.

She went into the kitchen to find one of the gingerbread house kits totally ravaged. When I say ravaged, I mean there was nothing left but the torn-open cardboard box and the shredded plastic wrapping. Tyson and Chloe—but mostly Tyson—had eaten the whole thing. Chloe was fine, but Tyson was bloated and sick.

Misha was dumbfounded. Although the cupboard that contained the kits was low to the ground, it had been months since she'd put them in there. She was surprised that the dogs were even aware of them, as they hadn't shown any obvious interest in the cupboard. In dismay, she banished Tyson and Chloe to the backyard.

Eventually, Misha grew tired of the pitiful faces staring back at her through the sliding glass door, and she let them back in. Chloe went straight to her bed and tried to lay low, but Tyson padded up to Misha and immediately vomited on the carpet.

"Shit, Tyson!" Misha yelled.

He just looked up at her as if to say, "I don't feel good, Mom. I know I could have done that outside, but I want you to join in my suffering."

Misha put him back outside and quickly steam-cleaned the mess. Chloe was allowed to stay inside, as she seemed fine.

When Misha thought it was safe, she let Tyson back in. He followed her around, miserably seeking comfort.

"I don't know what you want, Tyson. This is what you get!"

He responded by vomiting again.

"Oh, Tyson," she lamented in disgust.

Once again, Tyson was put outside, and the mess was steam-cleaned.

This cycle repeated twice again before the evening was over. For the next two days, Tyson was relegated to the garage, where his messes were more manageable. He wasn't even allowed to come inside to sleep at night. He was beside himself. Not only was he physically sick, but he was an outcast, as well. Chloe, on the other hand, never got sick at all.

Aside from when he was recovering from hip surgery, this was the worst I had seen Tyson. He was even more miserable than the time he'd had the bone removed from his stomach. You'd think an incident like this would change his behavior, but you'd be wrong. About a week later, Madison came into the kitchen to find Tyson trying to open the cupboard to get at the other gingerbread house kits. We finally gave up trying to store them and threw them away.

Although Chloe hadn't eaten much if any of the gingerbread

contraband, we assumed she had played a part in the caper. Later, this was confirmed by Tyson himself . . . in a manner I never would have thought possible.

45: BOBO PICASSO

Tyson prowls the empty cupboards in search of mischief.

R oughly at around the same time as the gingerbread incident, Tyson committed two atrocities involving paint. The first one, albeit the least diabolical of the two, was equally annoying.

We were in the process of remodeling the bathrooms, and the carpenter was painting the hall bathroom. Tyson was familiar with him and generally laid around in the living room when he was working. On this particular occasion, however, the smell of the paint was too interesting. Tyson decided to investigate. When the carpenter left the house to get something from his truck, The Asshole of Love decided to see what the paint-filled pan on the bathroom floor was all about.

Part of his investigation involved walking through the pan and paw-painting all over the paint paper. Sadly, the carpenter didn't discover Tyson's masterpiece until it had been extended down the hardwood stairs and into the kitchen.

I was at Madison's swim practice when I got a text message from the carpenter informing me of the problem. I sat there furiously picturing the nightmare I'd have to deal with when I got home.

That dog! I thought.

Fortunately, the carpenter was conscientious enough to try to clean up the mess before it really set in, and he was successful in mitigating much of the damage. He texted me again about a half hour later and advised me he had taken care of it. Man, was I relieved.

The only remaining issue was Tyson's painted feet. When I got home, Misha and I stuck him in the sink and cleaned him off, lecturing him about what a little shit he was. He just stood there, looking not the least bit guilty.

A few months later, we were in the process of painting the kitchen when Tyson committed an even more grievous "paintrocity." This one was a real doozy.

In anticipation of painting, we took everything out of the kitchen and removed the cupboard doors. There was a drop cloth draped over the kitchen table, upon which sat a two-thirds-full gallon paint can and a closed container of peanut butter.

While I wasn't looking, Tyson decided he wanted the peanut butter. He jumped up and pawed at the drop cloth until it slid off the table, bringing down both the peanut butter and the paint can. Because the lid on the paint can wasn't very tight, it popped right off and the contents poured all over the linoleum floor. The paint-splashed peanut butter container remained intact.

When I came in and discovered the mess, I was in utter disbelief. Thankfully, this time Tyson didn't walk through the paint again and track it all over—but still, there was so much paint! Quickly I began cleaning it up, cursing at Tyson with expletives unfit for these pages, to which he slinked away to lie in the sun.

It ended up taking an entire roll of paper towels to clean up the portion of the mess that hadn't already begun to dry. The remainder of the paint had either splashed up on the walls or set into the crevices in the linoleum. Misha ended up removing the paint in the crevices with paint thinner and a small wire brush, also cursing Tyson's very existence.

For a day or two, she would curse and scold him every time he came near. He'd retreat to his bed, tail between his legs and ears pinned back. Eventually, he'd build up enough courage to try again, and Misha would let him have it. When her anger had subsided, she allowed him to sit in her lap, and he was content.

We wanted to believe the whole ordeal might prevent him from getting into such mischief in the future, but we knew better.

Still, as much as Tyson's mischievous ways sometimes pissed us off, it never diminished our love for him. In some ways, I think it even added to his charm (the paint can incident notwithstanding!). We often said that if he were human, we would despise him. I think the fact he was a dog made his roguery endearing.

46: STILL A LOVE

With all the mischief he got into, you might get the impression that Tyson was more of an asshole than a love. This definitely was not the case. He was certainly willing to misbehave if it meant getting what he wanted, but most of the time what he wanted was to love and be loved.

The moment everyone was home from their days at work or school, his happiness was palpable. He'd usually be right in the middle of everyone, either begging to be picked up or, if he could get to you, giving you endless kisses. If Tyson was unhappy, he'd let you know, both with his very expressive face and by wandering off to be alone. Regardless, he was always authentic, and you knew exactly how he felt about you.

One of the great things about dogs is that you can always count on them to be happy to see you and ready to shower you with love. Tyson wasn't like that. Most of the time he was happy to see you, and he displayed no shortage of love, but it wasn't guaranteed. There were many times when I came home after a long day at work and he'd react as if he didn't care one way or the other. Ultimately, he'd cuddle up with me and let me know he loved me, but only if he was feeling it.

This just made the love he displayed all the more special. It wasn't just a matter of him acting on instinct. He made a conscious decision to let you know you meant a lot to him.

47: QUITE A SCARE

One afternoon in May of 2017, Tyson and I lay on the bed and settled in for what I hoped would be a quick and uneventful nap. It wasn't uncommon for Tyson to have dreams, during which his legs would twitch and he would let out short muffled barks. It was adorable. But just as I began to drift off, I was awakened by Tyson jerking around rapidly. It seemed too violent to be a dream, so I sprang up to check on him. He was having a seizure.

He convulsed violently as foam formed around his mouth and his wide-open eyes bulged. I knew there was nothing I could do but protect him from falling off the bed and whisper to him that he was going to be okay.

The thing was, I didn't know that he *was* going to be okay. I had no idea what was causing the seizure, and I didn't know how long it would last. At this point, he was at least twelve years old, possibly thirteen. The rational side of me realized that regardless of how it turned out, it could be the beginning of his last days.

Ever since our first couple of months with Tyson, I made the conscious effort to appreciate every moment with him. I knew our time together was special, and I was careful not to take any of it for granted. I also tried not to think about the fact it would inevitably come to an end. As I helplessly watched him seize, I was suddenly catapulted into the undeniable reality that he was getting old and may not be around too much longer.

This sad reality was overshadowed by the awful sight of my boy suffering before my eyes. It killed me to not be able to make the seizure stop. Mercifully, it lasted only thirty seconds, but it seemed like an eternity.

Afterward, Tyson lay there like he was drunk. I wiped the foam from his mouth and wrapped my arms around him, petting him softly and telling him how much I loved him. It only took about five minutes before he seemed to bounce back to normal. I was so relieved that I brushed aside the idea the seizure might be an indication of greater problems.

The next morning, I took him to the veterinarian to get him checked out. The vet examined Tyson's general health and took a blood test to check for signs of cancer. To our relief, the test was negative—but the vet suggested something else might be wrong, and the only way to rule out the possibility of a brain issue would be a prohibitively expensive MRI. She recommended putting him on a minimal dose of phenobarbital, which would hopefully prevent future seizures.

In the coming weeks, no more seizures occurred; it seemed the medication was proving effective. Tyson was his normal self, and we were heartened by the idea that our beautiful friend would hopefully be around a few more years.

I wanted to believe the seizure was nothing more than a fluke. If only this had been true.

48: REFRIED BEANS!

Not long after the seizure, Tyson had a short-lived but intense love affair with a refried bean can.

Misha had taken out the recycling, which involved carrying the recycle bin through the garage. In the process, she inadvertently dropped a mostly empty refried bean can, and it rolled under a bunch of construction debris from the bathroom remodel.

Tyson found it and carried it to one of his beds, which also happened to be tucked behind the debris. Later, Misha walked into the garage and heard the unmistakable sound of tender love being made.

No, I'm not talking about the sound of canine intercourse, or any other kind of intercourse, for that matter. I'm talking about the sound of precious, affectionate cooing that can only mean true love.

Misha began looking for Tyson and his mate within the debris. Soon she found him in the throes of passion, his head fully inserted into the can as he licked away its remaining contents. He continued to coo intensely as he savored every last morsel.

Moving quickly and quietly, Misha summoned Madison to enjoy the adorable spectacle of tenderness. They giggled soundlessly, trying not to disturb the lovers. Eventually, they decided to give Tyson and his beloved the privacy they deserved.

When he was finished, with his head covered in bean crust, Tyson slowly walked into the house, regretful that he would never experience such an amazing connection again.

49: GETTING OLD

Starting around the middle of 2016, Tyson had started showing signs of his age. The first thing I noticed was that he slept even more than he used to, and sounds that used to wake him no longer did. I'm sure this was a combination of his hearing waning and being generally more tired.

In the past, when I took him somewhere with me and left him in the car for a couple of minutes, the moment I remotely unlocked the car door, he'd pop up and put his front paws on the window. It was something I always looked forward to. Nowadays, he stayed fast asleep until I opened the car door and called out his name.

He'd also begun to hold his right front "probing" paw up a lot more frequently. We were managing the pain with medication, but the situation was certainly declining. Sometimes he limped on only his left paws. We called him our old bipod.

Tyson's age and slow decline were a sad and undeniable reality, about which I did my best to stay in denial. If I thought about it at all, I'd remind myself it was all an inevitable and natural process—that it was nothing to be sad about but rather something to embrace. It was easier said than done.

In the fall of 2017, we sold our house in Castro Valley and moved to Pleasanton. Madison's year-round swim team was in Pleasanton, and it had become clear she was going to be a dedicated swimmer for the foreseeable future. Eventually, her practices would become longer and there would be pre- and after-school practices several times per week. This would be impossible to manage living in Castro Valley.

The real estate market was so competitive in the Bay Area that sellers were not taking contingent offers, so we had to sell the house in Castro Valley before making offers on a new home. This meant we had to rent an apartment until we could buy. The process was no fun, but it was necessary, so we accepted it.

A day or two after moving into our interim apartment, Tyson

started squinting his left eye, obviously uncomfortable. We took him to the vet and were referred to a veterinary ophthalmologist who determined Tyson's lens had detached and was pressing against his cornea. This would ultimately cause glaucoma and blindness, not to mention that it was very painful. The lens had to be removed. The good news was that, although it would be blurry, he wouldn't lose sight in that eye.

The unbelievably expensive procedure was performed, and once again Tyson came home wearing the infamous cone of shame. He had sutures in his eye; the Elizabethan collar was necessary to prevent him from damaging or removing the sutures, thus preventing the eye from healing.

Within a few days, Tyson started squinting as if he was in pain. I took him back to the ophthalmologist. Sure enough, Tyson had found a way to damage the sutures. Another very expensive procedure had to be performed to correct the sutures.

There was good news and bad news: The procedure was successful, but Tyson was now mostly blind in his left eye. The doctor consoled me, pointing out that since Tyson didn't need to worry about predators in the wild, losing sight in one eye would be no big deal to him. I knew she was probably right, but it broke my heart.

My boy was really breaking down.

50: ANOTHER SCARE

Tyson had another seizure within only a couple of weeks of the second eye procedure. It was just like the first.

We were on the bed when it happened, and it lasted a torturous thirty seconds. A day later, he had yet another one. This time he was walking down the hallway when he started convulsing.

Madison and I watched it happen. Tyson skidded out of control and wound up in the bathroom.

Madison screamed.

Moving quickly, I shielded his head as he foamed at the mouth, eyes bulging.

"Come back to us, Tyson. Come back to us," I encouraged.

Madison sobbed, devastated. Once again, the seizure lasted a difficult thirty seconds.

The next day, I took him to the vet, who recommended that we increase the dosage on his phenobarbital—the dose we'd had him on for seven months leading up to this point had worked to prevent more seizures, but it was obvious some changes had to be made. Still hopeful that the episodes could be treated medicinally, we agreed.

Within only a few weeks, we purchased and moved into a home in Pleasanton, and Tyson's cone of shame was removed. We were settling nicely into the new house, and it had been a couple of months since Tyson's last seizure. Then, on a Thursday morning in early March of 2018, I woke up to Tyson seizing.

In terms of convulsions, the seizure was mild enough that it hadn't awakened us. Once I was awake, though, I realized what was happening. Tyson's head and mouth twitched, and foam oozed from his mouth. Although he was awake, he didn't seem to be alert.

This seizure was different. It didn't last thirty seconds. It went on and on. For all we knew, it had already been going on for hours.

We decided that I should rush him to the emergency vet clinic, but before I could get dressed to go, Madison woke up and came into the room. As Tyson's seizures continued, Misha told Madison that he was very sick—and that she should say goodbye to him now because he might not get better. I was thankful Misha told her this. I didn't want to think about the possibility, let alone verbalize it.

It took the vet most of the day to get the seizures to stop entirely. Since the phenobarbital was no longer preventing the seizures, an MRI was recommended to see if Tyson had a brain tumor.

The following morning, I picked him up and drove him to another veterinary clinic for the MRI and a spinal tap to determine the cause of the seizures. Misha and I had always said that if Tyson ever needed medical attention, no amount of money would stop us from trying to help him. Between the eye procedure, the MRI, and the spinal tap, we had spent somewhere in the neighborhood of $12,000 in just four months.

We didn't have this kind of money to spare, but there was no other option. He was our boy, our friend, our soul mate. We paid the fees without hesitation.

After the procedures, the doctor showed me a lateral image of Tyson's brain. Sure enough, there was a small tumor that was most likely causing the seizures. It was the conclusion that I expected, but what the doctor told me next was not.

Removing the tumor, the doctor said, was not an option. Doing so would cause severe brain damage. She also told me it was uncertain whether Tyson could recover completely from the seizures. Even if he did, he might only live six months to a year, and that would be with the help of chemotherapy to reduce the rate of the tumor's growth.

I don't know what I expected. I guess I was hoping for a miracle, that somehow they could either eliminate the tumor or find a way to manage it for another couple of years. The idea that Tyson most likely wouldn't be around for Christmas, if he survived at all, was a sudden and harsh reality. It was devastating, but I tried to remind myself that this was part of the cycle of life. I had known this time would come eventually. Still, none of that made it any easier. Sometimes life can really be the shits.

To make matters more difficult, that coming weekend Madison had an all-star swim meet in Carson City, Nevada. She had worked extremely hard to qualify for it, so skipping it was not an option. One of us—Misha or myself—would have to stay home, as Tyson wouldn't be able to come home from the vet until he was completely stabilized. Misha didn't feel comfortable driving through the snowy mountains, so we decided I would take Madison.

We left before dawn on Saturday to make it there by early afternoon for a scheduled practice and a dinner banquet. I didn't want to be away, but I also welcomed the escape. Madison slept soundly in the back seat while I listened to music and tried to keep a positive perspective.

The Four Tops played "Baby I Need Your Loving," "Bernadette," and "It's the Same Old Song." I followed that up with a triple-shot of The Temptations: "Ain't Too Proud to Beg," "Get Ready," and "Papa Was a Rollin' Stone." The music lifted my spirits, but all I could think of was Tyson. I feared he wasn't going to make it through the seizures, and I tried to mentally prepare myself. To this day, although I still love that music, I can't hear any of those songs without being transported back to that time on the road.

A three-hour road closure on the way to Carson City had us stuck on a scenic spot on Highway 88, but we were stuck nonetheless. There wasn't much to do besides play in the snow, for which we didn't have the best clothing, or sit in the car and keep warm . . . and think.

Madison and I played for a bit, but my feet quickly started to freeze and I went back to the car. Madison, being the spunky kid she is, was content to play in the snow far longer. We had no cellular coverage where we were, so calling Misha to check on Tyson wasn't an option. All I could do was sit and think. Even though I had Madison's company, I felt isolated and sad. Before I knew it, I was bawling my eyes out.

Madison was still playing outside but came running to the passenger door to see what was so funny. Apparently, she had never heard me cry before and thought I was laughing. The eager smile on her face melted into an alarmed frown, and she quickly walked back to the snowbank where she'd been playing.

I felt bad, but I needed the emotional dump, so I kept crying. When I was finished, I called Madison to come back to the car.

"Is it weird to see your dad cry?" I asked.

"Yeah."

"I know you haven't really seen me cry, but it's perfectly normal, you know? I really love Tyson."

"I know." The confidence in her voice put me at ease. "The Bobo's a rat!" she remarked.

"Yeah, he's quite a character."

We reminisced about some of Tyson's memorable antics. We

laughed as we lovingly shared his stories of mischief. I could tell Madison wasn't hurting like I was, but I think it did us both a lot of good nonetheless.

By the time the road finally opened, there was no way we were going to make it to the practice on time. We arrived in Carson City and got checked into the hotel with just enough time for a quick break before dinner.

I called Misha, who had good news. Tyson was improving, although they were having trouble getting him to eat. Misha had gone to the hospital earlier and fed him baby food, which he ate willingly. She told me she would soon be returning to feed him dinner. This was great news indeed!

The dinner was for the swimmers only, so I had to find my own accommodations. I wasn't in the mood to live it up, so I went to the hotel buffet and washed down a mediocre meal with a soda.

Misha called me up on FaceTime. It was cathartic to see her holding Tyson like a baby, although he looked so sad. She petted him softly and he buried his face in her neck, comforted by her touch. I told him how much we loved him as she offered him small amounts of baby food.

She said the doctor believed Tyson would make a full recovery from the seizures, and that he would be able to return home within the next couple of days. I was elated. After being prepared for him not to make it, he was coming home after all!

I knew we wouldn't have very long with him, but I was so thankful for whatever time we had left. We would cherish every moment!

51: SACRED TIME WITH OUR FRIEND

Tyson came home the following Monday. He was still in recovery mode, but by the middle of the week, he was back to his normal self. Like I said, I was always cognizant of how precious every moment with him was, but now my appreciation had increased tenfold. Every moment seemed like a special gift.

One memory that really stands out was sitting with him at Madison's swim practice, where he had always been a regular visitor. It was late afternoon, not long before dusk, and it was beautiful and brisk out. Tyson was sitting on my lap, looking around and seemingly appreciating the moment as much as I was. I felt engulfed in love and appreciation for my special, furry soul mate. I decided to capture this now-beloved moment with my phone.

Although the picture doesn't show it, I zipped him up in my jacket to keep him warm, his face sticking out like a baby kangaroo. One of the coaches walked by and asked if we had a new puppy. I told her Tyson was actually a senior dog, but that he'd hopefully be around a while.

I sure do wish he was a puppy again, I thought.

Another wonderful memory with Tyson was sleeping in on a Sunday morning in early April. He had snuggled up with me, and Misha was kind enough to take a picture of us as we slept. I woke up with my arm wrapped protectively around Tyson's warm, soft little body. This had happened many times throughout his life, but I savored the moment with all I had.

When I say Tyson was back to his normal self, this included his typically insatiable desire to eat. He also still probed with his "probing paw" and ended up hobbling around on two legs.

During one of these probing sessions, Tyson found something interesting in the bathroom garbage can. Apparently, he had sniffed and probed a bit too aggressively (I'm sure his blindness probably played a role too), and he ended up falling face-first into the can.

The can was deep enough, as well as narrow enough, that he couldn't get out—couldn't even get himself right side up. I was down the hall when I heard the horrific sounds of Tyson screaming in terror.

Assuming something awful had happened, I was relieved and found it quite humorous to see Tyson pay such a hysterical price for his dumpster diving! Still, it hurt my heart to hear him scream after he had been through so much, so I quickly rescued him. Misha later said I should have videoed the moment for posterity, and I kicked myself for not having done so.

Given Tyson's usual propensity for mischief, it was easy to pretend he hadn't been on his death bed such a short time ago. Of course, the bald spot on the back of his neck from the spinal tap was always a poignant reminder.

A similar incident occurred one night while we were sleeping. Tyson was lying under the covers at the foot of our bed and somehow got himself stuck between the footboard and the mattress. He let out the same horrific scream as before, jolting Misha and me out of sound sleep, but this one wasn't funny at all. It wasn't the result of his usual mischief, and it could only have resulted from him being disoriented.

Nothing like this had ever happened before, and Tyson's screams were so vulnerable and raw. It broke my heart.

Each night, Misha and I took turns getting up at one in the morning to give Tyson his medications. He would take them down enthusiastically because we wrapped them in peanut butter, but it was a very sad process. Administering medications throughout the day can easily become routine, but being jolted out of sleep to do so was a nightly reminder that our boy's health was anything but routine. I tried not to think about it that way, instead focusing on savoring even these moments, but it was painful nonetheless.

In the following weeks, other than the medications, things were pretty normal. Tyson was his mischievous, beautiful, loving self. Each night, he snuggled with us. He came to many of Madison's practices. He begged, even demanded, as many bits of food as I would give him.

He hovered around Misha as she made dinner just in case she dropped something. He greeted me with his signature low-key manner, vertical tail wagging slowly.

I was really becoming optimistic that maybe we'd be lucky enough to have him around for longer than the doctor predicted. Unfortunately, this wasn't to be.

52: SAYING GOODBYE

On the evening of Wednesday, April 18, 2018, Tyson had been resting in his crate. As I walked past him, I saw that he was now sitting up, but he was leaning against the side of the crate as if he couldn't stand on his own.

"I think Tyson might be having a problem," I told Misha.

"Yes, I know," she replied sadly.

Misha had already noticed but didn't want to say anything. I picked Tyson up and held him, trying to assess how alert he was. He wasn't having a seizure, but it was obvious he was impaired. He kept opening his mouth and making a really slow breathing sound as his mouth slowly closed.

We'd been giving him CBD oil made specifically for dogs in the hopes it might help with the tumor. My first thought was that maybe he'd gotten too big of a dose and was just really stoned. He was still alert enough to know I was there, and every time I came close and told him how much I loved him, he licked my face. I hoped his impairment had nothing to do with the tumor.

Throughout the night, Tyson's odd breathing pattern persisted, but he continued to give kisses. At around 5 a.m. we decided I should take him to the emergency clinic.

I told the veterinarian and technicians about the CBD oil, and they thought it was plausible that it might be causing the impairment. The vet said the popularity of CBD oil was so new that she didn't have much experience with it. At any rate, Tyson seemed miserable.

He stayed at the clinic all day, and another veterinarian called me in the early evening to tell me his condition was about the same as it had been when I brought him in. The doctor said he couldn't be sure yet whether the cause was the CBD oil or the tumor, but he was optimistic Tyson would improve overnight. We'd just have to wait and see.

I remember how optimistic I was. I felt terrible about the possibility of having given him too much CBD oil, but I really wanted to believe this was only a temporary setback.

All throughout the following day, I received status updates from the vet. They weren't good. Tyson's condition wasn't improving. In fact, he seemed to be deteriorating. Sometime around 3:30 in the afternoon, the doctor called me to say he believed the cause was the tumor, as the impairment would have abated by now if the CBD oil had been the cause.

Then came the hammer. The doctor suggested we come to the clinic—and depending on how Tyson's condition progressed in the coming hours, it might be best if he were put at peace.

I felt like someone had just kicked me in the stomach. My whole body tingled as I processed what the doctor said. Madison and I were in standstill traffic when I took the call, which was oddly comforting because it would delay our arrival to the clinic and the miserable reality that awaited us.

I called Misha and gave her the news. She immediately started crying. We agreed to meet at the clinic and, without further conversation, hung up. Madison, though greatly concerned, seemed to process the news with a calm understanding beyond her years.

When we arrived, the receptionist asked us to sit in the waiting area. I looked around at the sweet, cheerful, illustrated pictures of dogs and cats on the wall, and I was barely able to hold it together. I so badly wanted for the technicians to bring Tyson out to me like they had so many times before, full of vigor and personality, eager to get the hell out of there.

Soon we were directed to a treatment room, and a technician brought our boy to us. He was wrapped in a pee pad, as he was now incontinent. His eyes were glazed over, but he was aware of us. I held him like a baby, telling him how much he meant to us, how much joy he had brought, how much he had changed our lives for the better, how I would never be the same.

Tyson responded by licking me with as much enthusiasm as he was capable of. It seemed he was as aware of the significance of the moment as we were. I cried like a baby as I rocked him back and forth. Madison cried too, sweetly petting him.

When Misha arrived, she smiled and pleasantly thanked the technician for showing her to the room. As she shut the door and turned toward us, her smile quickly melted to anguish as she began to cry. She sat down, and I put Tyson in her arms. She sobbed as she held him close to her chest, telling him how much she loved him.

Before long, the doctor came in and we discussed our options. His opinion was that Tyson's condition was not going to improve; that what was best for him was that he be put at peace. As much as we hated to agree, we knew Tyson was suffering. The doctor was right.

We were brought into a cozy room with plush furniture, the lighting dim and warm. If I didn't know any better, I would have thought we were in someone's living room about to watch a movie. Each of us loved on Tyson and softly reminded him of his cherished place in our lives and hearts. As exhausted as he must have been, he still managed to acknowledge each of us with affectionate kisses.

Although we wanted to sit there with him forever, we knew we were only prolonging the agony. I notified the doctor that we were ready, and he came into the room. He was very compassionate, and he assured us that the whole process would be very peaceful for Tyson.

I looked over at my boy, who closed his eyes like it was now uncomfortable for him to keep them open. Misha said she would hold him until the process was over, but I couldn't bear to stay in the room.

I softly advised Misha and the doctor that I would wait outside. Madison decided to come with me. We each kissed him and said goodbye for the last time.

53: A SAD RETURN HOME

I exited the clinic, barely holding it together enough to say goodbye to the technicians. The moment we were outside, I started bawling. As tough as Madison had been until now, she also broke down. Neither of us cared that we were in a public place in broad daylight.

My body was numb as we drove home in silence. I kept trying to remind myself that Tyson was at peace and no longer in pain; that this was all part of the natural order of things. For his peace, I was thankful, but I felt like my heart had just been ripped out . . . that a beautiful part of me had just died.

When we got home, Madison quietly went to her room. After a few minutes, I poked my head in to check on her. Although she still seemed a bit somber, I was heartened to see her sitting on her bed, coloring. It was obvious that losing Tyson wasn't going to be as hard on her as it was on Misha and me. For that, I was grateful.

I lay down in bed and stared up at the ceiling, trying to process the fact I would never see Tyson again—that I would never see my beautiful Bobo, my Asshole of Love, my furry soul mate, my heartlight, again. Like anyone else my age, I had experienced my fair share of loss and heartache. I knew that the coming weeks, months, even years were going to be a slow process of acceptance and healing. I tried to simply be with this reality.

Soon, Misha came home. She seemed to be in her own numb world as she walked through the door. She held Tyson's collar in her hand. Seeing this delivered to me a dagger of pain and a poignant reminder of the finality of the situation.

She smiled at me sadly and said, "I love you, Tyson," as she set the collar down on the kitchen counter. We embraced, offering each other the support we would definitely need.

Although no one felt hungry, Misha ordered a pizza. What was normally a treat tasted like cardboard. Madison was still doing well, but Misha and I spent the remainder of the evening crying on and off.

By the time we went to bed, we were both totally exhausted and had splitting headaches. As we turned in, the absence of the cuddly warmth of Tyson's presence sent another dagger of reality through us.

As hard as it was to fall asleep, I welcomed the escape from the sadness of the day.

54: THE DAY AFTER

The next morning, I dragged myself reluctantly out of bed. I still had a headache. Misha was feeling no better. Together, we felt like we were recovering from the flu. I've never been one to force myself to carry on with my normal routine when I'm really hurting, so my plan was to just stay home and take it slow. I felt so sad and fragile. The thought of coping with the outside world seemed like a really bad idea. Misha and Madison also wisely stayed home.

We spent the day watching TV and moping around, but it seemed like the healthiest thing we could do. I spent a lot of time just sitting there, staring at the ceiling, thinking about Tyson. I thought about how lucky we were to have been blessed with him in our lives. I thought about how much he had opened my heart; how being his human had made me reconnect to and embrace the most sensitive and vulnerable parts of myself. I longed for him. I longed to know that he lived on.

Like so many people, I had always believed in a "higher power." Instinctively, it seemed, I knew there was much more to existence than just what we perceive here on Earth. I had also always been just fine not knowing what that higher power was.

During my childhood, I occasionally went to church with friends, but it never felt right to me. The dogmatic beliefs I was exposed to seemed unrealistic. I enjoyed the people, but I felt if I wanted to be a part of their community I would have to force myself to believe in what I viewed as a fairy tale. I'd felt this way from a very young age, probably around the age of six.

When I was in my early twenties, I explored several Christian religions. Again, although I would have loved to have been a part of the spiritual communities within these religions, I just couldn't find truth in them.

I was twenty-five when I met and fell in love with a woman who was very religious. In an effort to please her and her family, as well as to give religion another try, I studied her religion and tried to find truth in it. Not surprisingly, I found no such thing. Although we went so far as to get engaged, we ultimately broke up because she could not bring herself to marry someone outside of her faith. I was utterly devastated, and it took me a long time to recover, but I simply couldn't follow a religion I didn't believe in.

Don't get me wrong—I didn't (and don't) have anything against formal religion. I've come to realize that spirituality is a very personal endeavor. I believe that if one's relationship with a higher power, or lack thereof, brings them peace, then it is a worthwhile pursuit. That is, of course, as long as it isn't harmful to others.

While many nonreligious people may have specific spiritual belief systems, this was not the case for me. I had no defined beliefs about what happened to a person or animal when they died. Did they go to Heaven or Hell? Did they resurrect? Did they simply cease to exist? I had always thought it was absurd to think anyone could know this. For me, it made a lot more sense to believe that we continue to exist, but I felt being positive about the form of that existence was unrealistic. My peaceful spiritual paradigm consisted of an undefined higher power with an equally undefined afterlife.

Although this paradigm was very honest, it certainly had its downsides. For me, the loved ones in my life, whether friends or family, have always been what matters most. Sure, personal accomplishments are important to me, and leisure pursuits are an integral part of life, but none of that has much meaning without loved ones to share with. The fact I didn't have a defined belief system offering the promise of an afterlife where I'd be reunited with loved ones often made me sad, especially when I went to work as a police officer and faced the daily reality of the inherent dangers of the job—

the reality I might not make it home.

There were times when I went to work thinking, *Is it really worth it to do this risky job every day? If I were to die in the line of duty, no one would care except for my family and friends. I'd just be another statistic, and worse, I'd be dead—no longer able to be with my loved ones.*

I know these thoughts and feelings are very common, and I didn't think of them as a bad thing. They were just a part of a life I was trying to live as honestly, both in behavior and belief, as I could.

A good friend once said to me that she thought the point of life was to simply have more good days than bad. This resonated with me. I believe good days are those spent making a positive contribution, in whatever form that is. For some, it might be tending to a beautiful garden that brings them and others joy. For others, it might be taking care of the sick, or enjoying a fun day at the park and spreading good energy to others, or fighting a fire to protect life and property. What matters is that the day made a positive difference and that a person found happiness in this fact.

Trying to create positive days with loved ones at my side, even with my sometimes uncomfortable spiritual paradigm, is most certainly a worthy life pursuit, and it was one I was at peace with. I was living a good life, and I was making a positive difference in the world. That was good enough for me.

Like any other middle-aged person, I had lost my fair share of loved ones. All were sad losses, some devastatingly so, but I accepted them all as a natural part of life. Even with my undefined spiritual paradigm, I had little trouble making peace with them. I truly believed that my loved ones lived on, even if I didn't know exactly what that meant.

Losing Tyson was different. Obviously, I was in the midst of intense grief, and I knew this would only pass over time, but it was more than that. Even though I knew he had lived a good, long life, his death felt like a tragedy and not just a part of the natural order of things.

I knew that healing from Tyson's death would ultimately require me to accept it, but unlike my previous encounters with death, I was having an extremely difficult time doing that. At first, I didn't realize I was struggling so much with it. I just knew I was hurting, and that was to be expected.

After moping around the house for a few hours that first day, I went for a drive and visited with my childhood friend Mike Stansbury. Mike has always been an animal lover, and we went for a walk and he listened supportively as I talked about Tyson. I was thankful to have a good friend to lean on, one who knew what I was going through.

Mike reminded me that we had given Tyson a great life, and that Tyson had given *us* a great life too; that there was a whole lot to be thankful for, even though things were painful right now. He also assured me he'd be there for me if I needed him. Mike's support meant a whole lot, and it provided comfort that eased my pain, even if only a little.

Still, after only an hour or two at Mike's, I was emotionally exhausted. While my visit was therapeutic, I knew I needed to go home and hibernate, which was what I did.

The next day was a lot like the previous one, although I didn't feel quite as emotionally raw as I had the day before. I moped around the house for a few hours then went for a drive. This time I visited with a good friend, Elra Jensen, who is a bit of a mother figure to me. Elra is also an animal lover. We chatted over coffee. Needless to say, Tyson's passing was the topic of discussion.

During our conversation, we talked about the afterlife. I'd known Elra to be somewhat religious, so I was surprised when she said she thought our physical death was the end of our existence.

Although I hadn't been consciously thinking about the afterlife, I realized at that moment I had been struggling with it. Subconsciously, I had been hoping Elra would assure me not only that Tyson lived on, but that I would surely see him again. I was hoping she would give me the reassurance that my undefined spiritual paradigm couldn't.

Elra was very nurturing and supportive, and although my visit with her was certainly comforting, it occurred to me that I was spiritually unsettled. I knew that healing from Tyson's death wasn't going to be as simple as accepting it and allowing time to heal the wound. I thought, *You fool! He wasn't just your best friend. He was like your child. Did you really think you'd be able to just accept it and move on?!*

That afternoon, Misha and I sat together in our backyard, enjoying a glass of wine. I looked up into our neighbor's large tree and took comfort in the beautiful rays of sunshine beaming through the leaves and branches.

"Here's to you, Tyson!" we said as we held our glasses up and gestured toward the sunlight.

Misha shared a very moving experience she'd had the night Tyson died. She had awakened to the sound of Tyson barking at her from the side of the bed. She looked down and saw him jumping up, beckoning her to lift him up. She picked him up, surprised that she could actually feel him. As she softly placed him between us, he suddenly became weightless and disappeared. She was sure that he had visited her to let her know he was okay.

Misha was raised in a Christian family, and she still practices, so I was surprised when she told me that she believed that Heaven, whatever that may be, was very close to us; that Tyson was still very close to us.

Since this wasn't the depiction of Heaven I knew her church taught, I was both intrigued and comforted by her words. Misha had always been religious, but she was also a free thinker, and I had a lot of respect for her spiritual approach to life.

Hearing these words of hope was cathartic. It was then that I thought some spiritual exploration could be essential to my grieving process. I didn't know it yet, but my spiritual world was about to be turned upside down.

55: A FIRST STEP

That evening, I started searching the internet for books about coping with the death of a pet. I came across a book titled *Animals and the Afterlife: True Stories of Our Best Friends' Journey Beyond Death* by Kim Sheridan. This seemed like a book that might address some of my concerns, so I bought the Kindle version and began reading immediately.

I found it to be a wonderful book. It is both fascinating and compelling but also very uplifting. I highly recommend it to anyone, especially those coping with the death of a beloved pet. For me, the most poignant sections discussed the author's extraordinary experiences with animal reincarnation and animal communicators.

An animal communicator has the ability to communicate telepathically with both live and deceased animals. For some, this may sound completely ridiculous, and I totally get that. Before I read this book, I would have thought so too—believe me! However, it wasn't long before I had my own very real experience.

I was so compelled by the true stories in the book that I began to consider the idea of contacting an animal communicator.

What do I have to lose? I thought. *Clearly, I've got some angst about this whole afterlife issue. Maybe this can help.*

In the book, the author discussed several specific communicators, and I decided to contact one. I'll admit I felt kind of weird about it. I thought, *I'm seriously paying someone to talk to my dead dog. Am I losing it?*

But when I thought about it logically, it didn't seem all that strange. *After all,* I reasoned, *if there is an afterlife, which I'm fairly sure there is, why is it so absurd to think that some people might be able to contact deceased spirits?*

The bottom line was that I needed to make peace with the issue, and I thought this might help. I decided to go for it.

I scheduled an over-the-phone session with a communicator here in California. Initially, I was skeptical of doing a session over the phone. *How are they supposed to know if they're talking to Tyson if I'm physically far away?* I wondered.

Yet the more I thought about it, the more it made perfect sense. After all, if we were communicating with spirit, it seemed reasonable that geographic location was irrelevant.

I was certainly excited about the prospect of communicating with

Tyson, but I was skeptical as well. I very much wanted to believe that this was possible, but I wasn't going to be convinced by vague or common information. In the end, I decided to approach it with an open mind and see what happened.

The communicator had me send her a photo of Tyson, as well as a list of questions and messages I wanted to communicate. One of my messages was that we wanted Tyson to know how much we loved him and how much he had opened my heart. I also asked him if he would consider coming back to us . . . as in reincarnation.

When the session started, the communicator advised me that she didn't always connect with a pet, as sometimes they weren't ready to talk. Other times, she continued, she could communicate with them but they didn't necessarily have much to say. She stressed that I shouldn't feel hurt or discouraged if this turned out to be the case.

It seemed reasonable to me, but I was fairly sure that if animal communication were a real thing, Tyson would communicate loudly and clearly—and that he'd have plenty to say.

The communicator then put me on hold while she communicated with Tyson. After about five or ten minutes, she came back on the line and told me she had, in fact, communicated with Tyson. And he was talkative.

Among many things, he said that we were "his heart." He also said that he *was* going to come back to us. He said he would return as a small dog again, and that he wanted to be named Tyson again.

The communicator also connected with Chloe, our other dog, and reported that Chloe was okay with Tyson coming back because, while she knew we loved her, she knew Tyson was "the star."

There were other things said, but they weren't particularly memorable. For the remainder of the session, the communicator was very kind and patient, and I was thankful for her services.

After we hung up, I sat there contemplating what had been said. The statement about Tyson being the star was certainly accurate. This didn't subdue my skepticism, though. All one would have to do, I reasoned, was listen to me gush over how much we loved him to surmise he was a very special pet, and most likely the favorite.

The affirmation that he would reincarnate was comforting. It was also exactly what I wanted to hear, and as much as I wanted to believe I had just communicated with Tyson, I wasn't convinced.

Initially, I felt sadder and more confused than I had been before the session. Even though it was unfair to expect the communication to convince me of its legitimacy, I was hoping it would.

I tried to be honest with myself about what I wanted to achieve through the communication. Was I looking for proof of life after death? This seemed like an unrealistic order—but then again, what was the point in having the session if I didn't believe it was legitimate?

I knew I'd need to hear some very compelling information to actually believe it was true. In retrospect, it seemed predictable that the session would leave me unsatisfied.

I was still incredibly compelled by the accounts in *Animals and the Afterlife*, and I simply wasn't ready or willing to just dismiss the concept of animal communication. I knew my grieving process was now tied to my exploration of the subject. I decided to do a session with another animal communicator and see how things went.

The next day, I called and left messages for two other communicators. A few hours later, one of the communicators' assistants called me back. Although the communicator was ill and unavailable for a consultation, she didn't want me to wait and referred me to Sondy Kaska of Heart Gems Communication in Iowa City, Iowa.

I scheduled an appointment with Sondy for the following week. In the meantime, she had me send her two pictures of Tyson. One of them was of him licking Madison, and the other was a group photo of me, Tyson, Misha, Madison, and Chloe. In this photo, Misha is holding Tyson, and Madison is holding Chloe. With the photos, I also included the same questions and messages I had provided the previous communicator.

After I mailed the information, I tried as best I could to put it out of my mind.

A few days later, I received a call back from the other communicator I'd left a message for. She had been out of town when I first called. I figured I was already doing two sessions, so I might as well do three! We scheduled an appointment for that evening, and I provided her with the same questions and messages I'd given to the first communicator.

Unfortunately, this session also left me unconvinced. The communicator was compassionate and patient, but there wasn't anything said that couldn't have been guessed. There were also two discrepancies with the information I'd received from the first communicator. First, she said Tyson wasn't sure if he'd be coming back. Second, he said if he did come back, he wanted to be named Jordie.

Don't get me wrong. I'm not saying these first two communicators weren't legitimate or skilled. But Tyson was such a unique dog that I was hoping for information more specific to him.

I still had a week before my session with Sondy, and now I was more skeptical than ever. Although I remained hopeful the session with Sondy would be different, I wasn't expecting much. I began to consider that I might just have to accept Tyson's death without the comfort of knowing that he was okay.

I was deeply disappointed, but I was being honest with myself. In my heart, I believed he lived on, and I tried to focus as much as possible on how lucky we were to have had him in our lives.

56: TYSON'S URN

When Tyson passed, we opted to have him cremated and for his ashes to be placed in a beautiful urn with his name on it. A few days later, Misha called me in the middle of the day to tell me the urn was ready to be picked up. Although it was my day off, I had to pick Madison up from school and take her to swim practice, so I wasn't able to get the urn. Misha planned on getting it on her way home from work.

"I'm really dreading this," she said sadly.

For some reason, I foolishly didn't think receiving the urn was going to be a big deal.

"I know it's sad, but try not to think of it as him. It's only his remains, and it's a beautiful memorial that he deserves."

"I know, but I can't help it," she said.

I was a little apprehensive about receiving the urn, but I really thought I'd be able to compartmentalize my feelings over what I saw as just a physical object. Compartmentalization is something I have to practice regularly at work, so I figured I'd be able to shield myself in this situation as well. In retrospect, this was pretty naive.

When Madison and I got home, Misha was already there. I asked her if she'd picked up the urn.

"Oh, yeah," she said, on the verge of tears.

Together, we opened the box and pulled out the urn. It was beautiful, reverent, and totally devastating.

I looked at the engraved nameplate on the front, and an avalanche of emotion flooded over me. My baby had passed, yes. His physical life had ended, and I was well aware of this, but somehow seeing this physical representation of his remains was overwhelming. It was the sobering reality of his loss being brought down on us like a sledgehammer. Misha and I both started bawling.

"My baby," I cried.

We stood there holding each other and sobbing, the urn braced between us. It was an incredibly painful moment, but it was also beautiful. The love we felt for our boy was so pure and raw. If we had been able to compartmentalize our feelings, it would have been a loss for both of us, and for Tyson as well. As we embraced his urn, we grieved his loss, but we also honored his memory.

We put the urn in a drawer under the hallway shelf where Tyson's collar and picture were on display. I felt bad just tucking it away, but we just couldn't handle seeing it every time we walked down the hall.

Before he was cremated, the people who performed the service made an ink print of one of Tyson's paws. It was presented in a white envelope. I could see the print through the envelope, but it was almost two months before I could bear to remove it and look at it.

I didn't finally feel comfortable having Tyson's urn on display for about another year and a half.

57: A TURNING POINT

I started off the session with Sondy by sharing my experiences with the first two communicators. I admitted that while I was still open to animal communication, I was also quite skeptical. Sondy was understanding, and while she admitted she couldn't guarantee the session would eliminate my skepticism, she told me she had already made a connection with Tyson and hoped the information she had would be compelling.

My first impression of Sondy, and one that has proven consistent and accurate, was that she was compassionate, confident, and authentic. She also was and still is a practicing attorney, which gave me cause to believe she wasn't just some charlatan trying to make a quick buck.

I learned her method of communication was a lot like a translator facilitating conversation between two people speaking different languages. She would tell her client what the animal said, and would then tell the animal what the client said. Through this process, I also got the impression that the animal can often hear what the client is saying without her help.

After our opening conversation, Sondy advised me that she was now "tuning in" to Tyson. The first thing she said was, "He says he's the dog of mischief."

Well, you certainly can't get more accurate than that, I thought. But still, I reasoned, it could have been a lucky guess.

"He says that when he came to you, he had to be a tough nut to crack so that you'd fall in love with him." My skeptical brain quickly tried to regard this as another lucky guess, but I was also very impressed. "He says that his life mission was to open hearts."

"Well, he sure opened mine," I replied.

Sondy next described the differences in the relationships Tyson had with me, Misha, Madison, and Chloe. Sondy said that Tyson and I were soul mates—like a combination of best friends, brothers, or a father and son, with strong mutual respect.

She said that Tyson and Misha were equally close, but that their relationship hinged more on mutual adoration than mutual respect, although there was still great respect there. Sondy said that while Tyson and Madison certainly loved one another, he was not her dog—Chloe was. Finally, Sondy told me that while Tyson was fonder of Chloe now that he was in the afterlife, in life he'd had a "take her or leave her" attitude about her.

This was all one hundred percent accurate. Now I was pretty blown away. Nevertheless, I started thinking of ways Sondy could have learned these details—ways other than the fact she may have actually been communicating with Tyson's spirit.

I wondered if she could have deduced all that from simply looking at the two pictures I'd sent her. But no. In fact, one of the photos showed Tyson lovingly licking Madison, which wouldn't have given anyone the impression that Chloe was closer to Madison.

For the first time, my skepticism was being beat out by the simple accuracy and specifics of Sondy's communication. More than that, I began to feel in my gut that this was very real.

Encouraged, and without any premeditation, I said, "Tell me about his leg." I figured that, considering the specifics she'd already shared, identifying his leg issue wouldn't be a problem.

There was about a three-second pause before Sondy replied, "His right rear leg, correct?"

"Yes," I emphatically confirmed.

Intuitively, I was confident that she would know about his leg. But intellectually, I was surprised. I simply couldn't explain Sondy's accuracy without admitting that she must have actually been communicating with The Asshole of Love.

At this point, I was in a mild state of euphoria. For the first time in my life, I had an honest, empirical reason to believe that there was life after death. More importantly, I had an honest, empirical reason to believe that Tyson lived on.

Sondy told me that Tyson's leg seemed to have had a nerve issue. I explained to her about his damaged right rear hip, how he'd come to us with the injury, and that we were never sure if it was due to a traumatic event or a developmental issue. She advised me that he had been born with the problem.

I then asked her to tell me about his tail. After a few seconds, Sondy said she didn't see anything unusual about it. I described to her how it wagged vertically instead of horizontally, and she laughed out loud.

"How cute!" she said.

She then explained that the image Tyson was sending her was of a tail wagging quickly and horizontally toward his right rear leg. She said she believed he was trying to communicate that his tail had wagged vertically due to nerve issues in his leg, which were probably also related to his leg's development. It certainly made sense.

Since Tyson had said he and I were soul mates, I wondered if we had lived other lives together. Although Sondy quickly confirmed that we had, Tyson didn't share any details from this life, or lives. That didn't stop my mind from imagining. In that moment, I pictured myself on a farm or ranch surrounded by dirt roads, running around barefoot in overalls. Figuring this was a case of my imagination running wild, I dismissed it. Still, it gave me a feeling of comforting warmth.

"He says that he took great pleasure in causing trouble and making it look like Chloe did it," Sondy said.

Immediately, I thought of all the times we'd wrongly blamed Chloe for tearing open my backpack to get to my protein bars, when in fact Tyson had been the culprit. And, of course, who could possibly forget the gingerbread house incident?

"Can you ask him about the gingerbread house?" I said.

"Oh, that was quite the project," Sondy replied. "Chloe was involved, but Tyson was definitely the mastermind."

"We always suspected that Chloe had helped with that one!"

My final question was, of course, whether or not Tyson would come back to us. Sondy said that Tyson wasn't sure yet. She got the distinct impression that he *wanted* to return, and once again as a small dog so that he could be held and cuddled.

As we concluded the session, I knew it had been a turning point for me.

"I think you've made a believer out of me," I appreciatively told her.

Sondy humbly expressed her pleasure at being able to help me and Tyson, and she invited me to reach out to her anytime I needed her.

After we hung up, I sat there processing what was said. I wasn't terribly surprised when my skeptical brain tried to elbow its way into my thoughts and convince me that, while Sondy had been sincere, she hadn't really been communicating with Tyson. She had just made some very lucky guesses.

Deep down inside, however, I didn't believe this was the case. What made the most sense to me was that she *had* been communicating with him.

I felt so much love and appreciation for my furry little soul mate. I knew that he was okay and was, in fact, thriving. I knew we were still connected and that he was still playing a huge role in my life, helping me grow and continuing to open my heart.

I felt I had just embarked on a spiritual journey that would undoubtedly bring a great deal of peace. I didn't know what that would look like, but I was finally ready to find out.

58: MEDITATION

So there I was with a brand new spiritual perspective. Actually, I was exhausted. This shift was very exciting, but it was also challenging. My cynical, skeptical mind was being overruled by the compelling information Sondy had shared, but I'd be lying if I said there wasn't a bit of an internal battle going on. The question was what should I do now?

A friend gave me the name of a spiritual medium he was acquainted with. Although he'd never had a session with her, he told me she'd been guided into mediumship through some life-changing metaphysical experiences.

While I was certainly interested, I just didn't feel ready. I was still trying to process my experience with Sondy and adjusting to a brand new spiritual paradigm. I had enough fodder to digest for the time being.

I looked for online courses on spiritual development that I could do on my own. Not only did I have a very busy schedule, but I also felt more comfortable keeping it a private process. Through my searching, I was introduced to meditation, which is essential to connecting to your higher spiritual self.

The idea, in a nutshell, is that you sit in a quiet room without distractions and block out all conscious thought. This allows you to become consciously aware of your subconscious because your busy mind is no longer blaring it out. It sounds pretty simple, but it takes practice. I won't get into meditation techniques here—only to say that it's a great way to promote physical, mental, and emotional healing, and I would definitely recommend it to anyone.

Initially, I was more interested in connecting to my higher self and gaining metaphysical insight than I was in the health benefits. Every day, I would spend about twenty minutes trying to "successfully" meditate.

I would sit there in silence, desperately trying not to think. Like most anyone who has ever tried it, I found that my mind constantly wanted to go at a hundred miles per hour, creating thoughts about anything and everything. And I do mean everything—from what I would eat that night to when I needed to leave to pick up Madison from swim practice to how much I missed Tyson, even trying to solve frustrating problems at work. My mind was always moving.

Gradually, I got better at quieting my mind and also at gently pushing away the thoughts that did pop up. Still, though, I wasn't experiencing any discernible connection to my higher self or any profound metaphysical insights.

Mostly, I just sat there killing time. At least that's what it felt like. Still, I knew Tyson had given me a beautiful gift by communicating with me through Sondy. It didn't make sense that this would happen without a significant purpose, so I kept up my daily routine despite its seeming futility.

Before long, I gave up on trying to "successfully" meditate, instead simply being open to whatever the universe had to offer me. It was a relief to not feel the pressure of trying to have some grand experience, and the process became more relaxing and enjoyable. I began to often feel a vibrant, loving energy flowing through me, and it always left me feeling more at peace and refreshed.

Although I never had any grand visions, occasionally I felt the physical sensation of a loving presence standing very near. If you're curious to know what this felt like, cover your eyes and have a friend stand close to you. You'll find that you can physically sense them. I could physically feel the spiritual presence, and on an emotional and intuitive level, I knew it was positive and loving.

One of the benefits of meditation for me has been becoming more cognizant of the importance of my spiritual place in the world, as well as that of others. My daily practice is my daily "tuning in" to what really matters, and allowing my spiritual being to take over. It always leaves me with a fresh, healthy perspective.

I first noticed the positive impact it was having on my day-to-day life during law enforcement interactions at work. As a parks police officer, I was often charged with issuing citations to visitors for having their dogs off-leash. Although leash laws play an important role in maintaining safety and quality of life—as well as protecting park resources—many visitors found them to be petty and frivolous. And they weren't afraid to tell me so. I once had a citizen escalate a simple dog-off-leash contact to the point where I ended up taking them to jail!

Anyway, one day while I was patrolling a trail within a strict resource protection area, I issued citations to four people in a period of thirty minutes. Three out of the four were hostile toward me. This wasn't unusual. What was unusual was my inner response.

I would always approach people in a friendly manner, and I generally ignored any insults or negative comments. Like most cops, I developed a thick skin, and I simply put up a mental wall. On this occasion, however, I observed that my perspective had shifted.

As I spoke with each of these individuals, I was firm, but inside I felt a certain level of warmth toward them as opposed to the detached toughness I usually felt. This was likely evident to them as well because each of them became reasonably friendly, albeit a little bummed, by the end of the contact. One lady was so mad at first that she was swearing like a truck driver. But by the end of our interaction, she asked me if she could give me a hug. I obliged.

Meditation was and has continued to be a wonderful first step into a richer, more spiritual life for me. The experience of communicating with Tyson through Sondy had given me loving evidence that we are spiritual beings having a human (or canine!) experience.

It was just the catalyst I needed to delve into this peaceful world. It certainly was a gift. A beautiful gift, indeed.

59: A PAW PRINT ON MY SOUL

About a month and a half after Tyson passed, I was finally emotionally ready to open the envelope containing the paw print that was made prior to his cremation. Removing it from the envelope stung, but I felt so much reverence for my boy that I was thankful to have it. After all, it seemed to me that this very paw print had been stamped on my soul. As a symbol of this, I decided to have it tattooed on my right shoulder.

A couple of weeks later, we went on vacation to Maui and I had the tattoo done at a parlor in Lahaina. Before I went in for the tattoo, I meditated, focusing on establishing communication with Tyson. I asked him to please be with me as it was done.

The tattoo parlor had a large lobby area, and there were about four other people sitting on a couch. One of them had a white service dog with her that looked like a Lab mix. As I approached the reception counter accompanied by Misha and Aunt Pam, the dog focused in on me like I had potatoes growing out of my ears.

It continued to do so with undivided attention for what seemed like a very long time—and although Misha and Pam were there with me the entire time, the Lab never paid any attention to them. In my secret heart, I hoped that meant Tyson was there with me and the dog was seeing him.

Brian, the tattoo artist, greeted me in a not-entirely-friendly manner. He was covered in tattoos and piercings, and I guessed my fairly conservative appearance made him think I was someone he wouldn't be able to relate to. But when I told him why I was getting the tattoo, and about some of the metaphysical experiences I'd had since Tyson's death, we clicked nicely.

The tattoo came out with perfect detail, including the ink-drop imperfections. Every morning when I brush my teeth, I look at my good friend's paw print and take a quick moment to remember him and be thankful for the impact he's had on my life and soul.

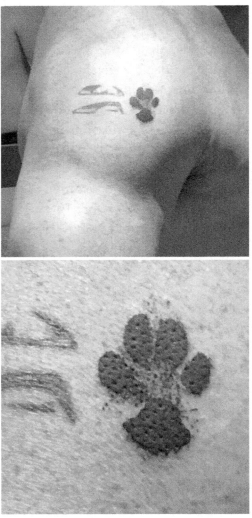

He put his paw print on my soul. I put his paw print on my shoulder.

60: EXCITASNEEZE

Not long after I got the paw print tattoo, Misha and I were watching TV and having dinner at our coffee table.

Chloe came up beside me to beg for scraps, which was normal. As Misha often said, I was "the weak link," which meant I was always willing to share a nibble here and there.

What was unusual about this instance was that Chloe suddenly began doing something only Tyson used to do—an odd quirk we'd affectionately named the "excitasneeze."

This was when Tyson would sit at someone's feet as they were eating, staring at them and sneezing over and over excitedly as if each sneeze would bring him closer to receiving his edible reward.

Misha and I looked at each other, eyebrows raised, and simultaneously said, "That was weird!"

Chloe was much more reserved about her begging, sitting quietly and staring, and if she'd ever had an excitasneeze episode before, we'd never noticed.

"I wonder if Tyson just paid us a visit," I said.

I'd read that it was possible for the spirit of an animal to temporarily occupy a body, but I wasn't sure I believed it.

"You never know," Misha replied, still marveling at Chloe's behavior.

To this day, Chloe has never repeated the excitasneeze.

Once, about a year and a half later, she sneezed out of excitement when we were taking her for a walk, but it wasn't near as intense or distinctive as Tyson's beloved display.

Sondy eventually confirmed for me that Tyson had, in fact, paid us a visit.

61: COFFEE WITH LOVED ONES

Some months later, I had a session with Lisa Silverman, the spiritual medium I'd been referred to by a friend. Before we set up an appointment, Lisa and I spoke by phone. She told me she had been psychic her entire life, but that she'd "stayed in the closet" for fear of ridicule. Only recently, following a life-changing metaphysical experience, had Lisa begun to work as a medium. She did this because she felt she could use her gift to help others. I was heartened to learn she owned a successful interior design firm, which offered indication to me that she, like Sondy, wasn't just trying to make a quick buck.

During the initial conversation, Lisa asked me what I wanted to achieve with our session. I told her that Tyson's death had started me on my spiritual journey but didn't tell her much more beyond that. Lisa had specifically asked that I not tell her any details about Tyson or his character. She didn't want to have any biases.

Finally, I told her I really didn't know what I wanted to achieve with the session, that it was something I saw as a kind of exploration. I soon found myself blown away by the things Lisa was able to see.

"Tyson is with you and your family all the time," she said.

This was certainly comforting, and I believed it, especially after the excitasneeze episode.

"Do you have Tyson's collar out on display?" she asked. "Like on a desk or a table?"

"Yes, I do." I had put his collar on display under his portrait within days of his passing.

"Is it hanging from something?"

"No, it's slipped under an easel, which holds his portrait."

"Are you sure it's not hanging from it? It looks like it's hanging."

I knew for sure it wasn't hanging, because at least once a day I pulled his collar from under the easel and kissed it. "No, it's only slipped under."

"Okay," Lisa said. "Well, he wants you to know that he really appreciates you having it on display." She then quickly changed the subject. "Did you have a childhood friend that passed while you were in high school? Someone with blond hair?"

"Well," I said, "I had an ex-girlfriend who passed during our sophomore year of college, but she had red hair."

"No, this isn't her. Huh . . . Just so you know, there are several people here that want to speak with you. I'm telling them they have to wait until our session next week."

I was intrigued. "Cool," I said, feeling it something of an understatement.

"Please try not to think too much about the session between now and then, because I will actually pick up on it, and it'll drive me nuts."

"Okay," I said, "no problem."

The moment we hung up, I walked to the hallway and looked at Tyson's portrait, easel, and collar. Looking at it now, if I hadn't known any better, I might have thought it was hanging from the back of the easel. I pulled it out and kissed it for good measure and to make sure it was not, in fact, hanging.

When I told Misha all about my conversation with Lisa later, she said, "That's interesting. I thought the collar *was* hanging from the easel."

Needless to say, I was a bit blown away by all of this. While I knew some people might choose to display their deceased dog's collar, it seemed fairly unusual—just as it seemed unusual for Lisa to mention the collar unless she was actually seeing it with her mind. Lisa seemed to be very much the real deal, and I was excited to see what information she'd receive.

The following week, I met her at her home as planned. Even though I had looked forward to the session with excitement, I'd done a good job of not thinking much about it, as she requested. I really wasn't expecting anything earthshattering, but I did hope Tyson would come through again. I missed him so much.

Nothing about Lisa or her home matched the stereotype of a spiritual medium typically promoted by the media and Hollywood. Her home was warm and welcoming, as was she, and if you were to see her on the street you definitely wouldn't think she spoke to spirits!

We sat down in her living room and, after a few pleasantries, she told me that there were spirits ready to chat.

"Did you have an uncle who passed when you were in high school or in your early twenties?" Lisa asked.

My Uncle Mark had passed in 1990 when I was sixteen. He had suffered from Hodgkin's lymphoma for the last five years of his life. He and I had always had a good relationship. He was a big movie buff and had taken me to see *The Empire Strikes Back*, *Return of the Jedi*, *First Blood II*, and *Aliens*, just to name a few. Mark had also been a very talented guitarist. The last time I saw him, he was in the ICU at Stanford Hospital in Palo Alto, hooked up to a bunch of machines. I remember it vividly because it was such a shock to see him like that. I had immediately started crying and had to leave the room to regain my composure. He died shortly thereafter, only in his mid-thirties.

I told Lisa that Uncle Mark had died when I was sixteen, but I didn't tell her how.

"Was he a real character?" she asked.

Uncle Mark was, indeed, quite the character—he was very theatrical, always cutting up and being the life of the party. "Yes, he sure was," I confirmed fondly.

"Did he die tragically?"

"Well," I said thoughtfully, "I wouldn't necessarily call it tragic. He died of Hodgkin's disease at a very young age. It was really sad."

"No," Lisa said. "No, he didn't. He died of something AIDS-related."

Her declaration floored me. Both my mom and dad had suggested in the past that Mark might have died of AIDS. Although Mark had never admitted that he was gay, after his death both Mom and Dad told me they believed he most likely was. I'd never really thought much about it, though. He was just my Uncle Mark. I didn't care if he was straight or gay.

"Well," I told Lisa, "although he never admitted it, many people thought he was gay, and some thought he might have died from AIDS."

"Yes," Lisa said confidently. "He was gay. He's asking if you thought he was. He says he always felt a special connection with you, and he thinks your bond would have grown much stronger if he had lived."

This definitely rang true to me. I thought Mark and I would have enjoyed meeting for beers and talking about life. Years after Mark's death, I earned a degree in film and later made a number of short films, a sitcom pilot, and a feature film. I also worked as a production assistant on the first *Men in Black* film and the entire last season of *Married... with Children*. I know Mark would have loved being a part of my films, and he would have been ecstatic for the opportunity to come to the set of a real Hollywood movie or television show.

"Can you ask him if he remembers the time when he let me drive his big ol' tank of a car when I was first learning to drive?" I asked. Mark had been pretty sick during this time, but that didn't stop him from being supportive.

"Yes, he remembers it fondly."

"I really appreciated him doing that for me. It's a great memory."

"He says that he lived with a lot of mental torment but that he's worked through his issues. He wants everyone to know that he is at peace now. Physically, he's in his twenties."

This really warmed my heart. While Mark was always a genuinely nice person and a great uncle, he was prone to intense temper tantrums. I only witnessed one, but I'd heard about many more. In retrospect, this was understandable. Not only was homosexuality far less accepted during the 70s and 80s, but Mark had been raped while playing in a band in Hawaii. I won't share details here, but this experience would have caused extreme trauma for anyone, let alone someone who was already struggling with their sexual identity. It was wonderful to hear that he had found peace.

"I will pass that on to everyone," I said. "That will make them happy."

"So your mom was one of three kids?" Lisa asked, seemingly switching gears.

"No. There were four kids in her family."

"Oh, okay. So three siblings."

"Yes."

"Two girls and your Uncle Mark, correct?"

"Yes."

"One of them is still alive, and one of them has passed?"

"Yes, my Aunt Anna is still alive, and my Aunt Chris has passed."

It was truly mind-blowing how accurate Lisa was.

"Chris is here with Mark," Lisa said.

"Hi, Chris!" I said, waving at the air all around Lisa. I figured Chris must be somewhere near Lisa, so waving in her general direction felt appropriate.

"Were they really close?" Lisa asked.

"Yes." Mark and Chris were the middle two kids, and they'd always shared a close bond.

"They're still very close," Lisa said, indicating their existence in the afterlife.

"That's great to hear."

"Does your mom's maiden name start with a J?"

"No, her maiden name is Bradshaw."

"Huh. I keep seeing the letter J."

I pondered what the J might be for, but I couldn't think of anything.

"Your Aunt Chris says that she had problems with drugs throughout her life and that it ultimately killed her."

"Yes, she did. She actually died from a methamphetamine overdose."

"She says that she tried to find peace through men."

"Well, it sure seemed that way. She was married at least five times."

Aunt Chris had come over to our house a lot when I was young. She was always a fun person. She'd take me, my brother Chason, and my sister Andrea to the beach and let us spend the night at her house. After her third divorce, she didn't come around much anymore, and I think this was when the drug issues really intensified.

When I was in college, during Chris's fifth marriage, she had a son named James. It was something of a miracle because she was in her forties by then and had never been able to get pregnant before. We all considered it a miracle, especially with all of the drug use. She was a devoted and caring mother, but ultimately this marriage didn't last either and she turned back to drugs.

"Can you thank her for all the times she baked us chocolate chip cookies and took us to the beach?" I asked.

"She says she was always up and down, up and down. She's showing me a wave motion with her hand."

"Yes, she definitely was."

"She says she's at peace now, and she's physically in her twenties, which was her healthiest time. Are you sure no one has a name that starts with a J? I keep seeing the letter J in neon lights."

The phone rang, and Lisa looked to see who was calling. "Sorry, I have to take this. I'll be right back," she said as she walked into her office.

While she was there, the obvious suddenly occurred to me. The J was for James! Chris was trying to talk about her son, James.

As soon as Lisa returned, I told her. "I think the J is for Chris's son, James."

"Yes! That's it!" Lisa exclaimed. "Chris has a son named James. She says thank you for realizing it." She paused for a second then asked, "Is he around twenty-five or so?"

"Yes, that's about right. He was born in 1994."

"She asks that you tell James that she is with him a lot. And she asks that you check in on him because she thinks you could be a positive influence on him."

"Of course. I'd be happy to. I haven't seen him for a long time, but I'll reach out to him."

My Grandma Anne, my mom's mom, had died of leukemia just a couple of months before Uncle Mark passed. Naturally, I hoped she was there with Uncle Mark and Aunt Chris.

"Is my Grandma Anne with them? She was their mom."

Lisa paused for a moment. Then she said, "Yes, she is, actually. But she's kinda standing in the background. I don't know if she wants to talk. Would you like to speak with her?"

"Yes, absolutely, if she's willing."

Grandma Anne was a great lady, but she, too, had her demons. Most of the time, you couldn't find a warmer and more loving person, but she also suffered from depression. When she was down, she was like a different person. For most of my life, I only knew the warm side of her, but when my parents divorced, I saw a very bitter side of Grandma.

Mom was convinced that Dad had cheated on her, although this wasn't true. Mom's dad, my Papa Ed, had cheated on Grandma Anne quite a bit, ultimately leading to their divorce. Watching Mom in so much pain during the divorce seemed to make Grandma Anne hate Dad.

Because I always defended Dad when Mom badmouthed him, a rift formed between Grandma Anne and me. She wasn't hateful toward me, but things weren't as warm as they had been.

The sad part was that the leukemia took her before we ever had a chance to grow close again. I hoped she wasn't standing in the background because she thought I wouldn't want to talk to her.

Lisa advised me that Grandma Anne was coming forward, which was a relief. "Did she work retail?" Lisa asked. "Because she's showing some kind of sales counter."

"Yes, she worked at the cosmetics counter at Gemco."

Visiting her there with Mom was one of my earliest memories. Mom bought me a pack of Juicy Fruit gum, and, on the way home, I accidentally smeared it into the upholstery of her Volkswagen Bug.

"She's quite attractive and voluptuous, and she says she loved men."

"Yes, she was a pretty lady, and she was also very voluptuous," I laughed. "My understanding is that she did love men, and she loved to go out dancing."

"I'm getting the sensation of being kicked in the stomach," Lisa said. "Did she get cheated on a lot by her husband?"

"Yes, my understanding is that my Papa Ed cheated on her quite a bit."

"She says that she passed on mental illness to her children."

"I always thought their issues might have been partially genetic, so that makes sense."

"She says that after her divorce, she wanted to find a man to take care of her. She married a second husband who loved her very much."

"Yes, my Papa Stu."

This was really touching because Papa Stu was a wonderful man. He and Grandma Anne were already married by the time I was born, so I considered him to be my grandpa. He did take good care of her, and he loved her very, very much.

He was a warm person, but he was also a disciplinarian. I was a particularly willful kid, so he and I sometimes butted heads. I always knew he loved me, though.

I have fond memories of Papa Stu, who was a big fan of western wear, taking me to get my own cowboy hat and boots, and making me a bike lock out of spare chain and an old padlock he had in his garage.

Sadly, he died of lung cancer when he was only fifty-four. Grandma Anne's heart was broken, and I don't think she ever really got over it.

His was my first encounter with human death. I was nine years old, and it affected me deeply.

In the following years, I had several vivid "dreams" where he'd come to me and we hugged as I cried and told him how much I loved and missed him.

I no longer believe those were dreams. I believe they were spiritual visitations.

"She says that he loved you very much."

It warmed my heart to hear. "He was a great man."

"She says that she is very much at peace and happy now. Physically, she is in her forties, which was her best time." She had been married to Papa Stu during her forties, so this certainly rang true.

Talking to Grandma Anne through Lisa brought up a lot of thoughts and memories. I remembered one particular post-divorce argument Mom and I had while Grandma Anne was visiting. Mom was complaining about what a horrible heel Dad was and how he had most definitely cheated on her. I, of course, wasn't having it, and I staunchly defended him. Grandma Anne was infuriated, and I'll never forget the look of hatred on her face when she told me, "Your dad is a son-of-a-bitch!"

She might as well have punched me in the gut and broken my nose. I was devastated. I had heard Mom saying equally heinous things about Dad since he left, but hearing Grandma Anne say it was more than I was willing to take.

Enraged, I screamed, "FUCK YOU, BITCH!!!!"

Grandma Anne just looked at me with an expression of sheer disgust, as if to say, "Fitting behavior from a horrible grandson."

I stormed out of the room. I was furious, hurt, and ashamed. I couldn't believe I'd been so disrespectful to my grandma. I had always regretted that fight, but neither one of us had ever apologized for the things we said. I asked Lisa to tell her I was very sorry for saying those awful things. Lisa did, and Grandma Anne's response gave me peace.

"She says that you don't need to apologize. She was wrong to say those things about your dad, but she was triggered by the situation. She is proud of you for standing up for your dad because he is a good man."

"Still, I'm sorry for the things I said."

"She's proud of the man you've become, and she thinks you are a great daddy. She'll be available to help you if you need her."

Hearing this was beautifully cathartic. I had never regretted standing up for Dad, but I had always wished Grandma Anne and I could have talked about it and cleared the air. For thirty-one years, I had thought of her as someone from whom I was estranged. I had always loved her and had warm memories of her, but those memories also brought with them regret that we ended things on a sour note. I could finally let it go knowing that Grandma Anne and I were all good, and she was watching over me.

Lisa asked, "Is there anything else you want to say or ask?"

I couldn't think of anything more. "Nothing right now," I said. "Please tell them that I love them very much and look forward to seeing them again."

"They know." Lisa paused for a moment. Then she giggled. "Oh, your Uncle Mark is being sassy. He really is a character."

I laughed. This was just like Mark. As if to punctuate his sassiness, I suddenly caught a flash of Uncle Mark in my mind's eye. It was only for a split second, but it was so spontaneous and real that it didn't feel like anything I'd imagined. I believe now that I was seeing his spirit.

"Okay," Lisa said. "I'm going to go ahead and thank them and let them go."

I looked up into the air. "See you soon, Mark, Chris, and Grandma Anne."

After making such a strong connection with them, I'd have expected to have difficulty saying goodbye, but I didn't. It was clear to me that we were still very much connected and I would see them again. I wasn't sad. I felt like celebrating.

"Now," Lisa said, "let's move on to the elephant in the room. Which, of course, is your dog. He's been waiting patiently."

"Hi, Bobo!" I said, ecstatic to hear that he had shown up.

"He wants to reiterate to you that he appreciates you having his collar on display."

"Of course. We love him so much. He's our boy."

"Do you have his leash hanging on a hook?"

"Yes." We still keep his leash hanging on one of the hooks on our hall tree. These days we use it for Chloe.

"Do you use it to walk your other dog?"

"Yes."

"Yeah, he's noticed. He's okay with it."

"I only use it because I like the color better. I can go back to using Chloe's."

"No, he's good with it. He says that the two of you are very much soul mates, and he's still with you all the time."

This was very affirming, since Sondy had said the same thing.

"He was Misha's dog first, right?"

"Well, I was there from the beginning, but yeah, Misha originally adopted him from a friend."

"Oh, my God, he is so sweet," Lisa said. Tears began to pour from her eyes. "I'm sorry about the tears. Animals tend to get to me. He says that he came to Misha in order to get to you."

This moved me, too, and I began to well up. But it didn't seem right to me. Tyson had absolutely adored Misha. It sounded to me like he was saying he didn't love her as much as he loved me.

"But he loved her every bit as much as he loved me," I said.

"Oh, absolutely, he did. He loves her very, very much. But his mission was to be with you."

"Well, he opened my heart, that's for sure."

"What is your other dog's name?"

"Chloe."

"Was he kind of indifferent toward her? Like he got along with her but he could kinda take her or leave her?"

"Yes, that is exactly right."

"He cares for her more now that he's gone." Lisa paused for a moment, then she asked, "Was he very masculine?"

"Oh, yeah. He was *very* masculine. He had a real swagger about him."

"But was he also kind of frail? Because I'm getting pain on the right rear side of his body that moves all the way up to the front right."

After the accuracy Lisa had already displayed, I wasn't surprised that she would know about his leg, but it still bowled me over. It seemed unlikely that she would juxtapose frailty with masculinity—unless, of course, she was really talking to Tyson.

My skeptical mind was pretty much shut down at this point. I proceeded to explain about Tyson's leg and how he had compensated by putting extra weight on his right front paw, which caused it to become arthritic. I also explained that we hadn't known if the hip had been damaged by an injury or if it was a developmental issue.

"No, he was born with it," Lisa confirmed.

"Can you ask him if he will reincarnate and come back to us?"

"Sure." Lisa paused again for a few seconds. "He says that he'd like to come back, but he isn't sure if or when."

This was disappointing to hear, but I wasn't surprised. Sondy had told me the same thing.

At this point, the session had gone nearly two hours, twice as long as we'd originally scheduled. As we wrapped things up, it occurred to me that I forgot to ask about the tattoo.

"Before we finish," I said, "can you ask him about the tattoo?"

"Are you gonna get a tattoo of him?" she asked, touched.

"No," I said with a mischievous smile.

I was surprised Lisa had gotten this wrong. Maybe she had lost some of her objectivity after experiencing all the love that had been communicated through her. But then she hadn't even taken a second to communicate with Tyson before she spoke.

It was as if Tyson had clued her in. "Oh!" Lisa said enthusiastically. "You got his paw print tattooed on you!"

I pulled up my sleeve and confirmed what she already knew.

"Yeah! That is so sweet!" she said approvingly.

On that positive note, we said goodbye to Tyson and ended the session. Lisa gave me a hug and assured me that she'd be there for me as I progressed spiritually. When I asked her how much I owed her, she charged me only for the originally agreed-upon hour. Incredibly gifted *and* generous!

As I drove home, I processed all of the information that had been shared. Needless to say, I was struck with how accurate Lisa had been, and I couldn't think of any reasonable explanation as to how she'd known so much about Mark, Chris, Grandma Anne, and Tyson . . . other than she had actually been in communication with them.

What really resonated about the whole experience was the feeling of connection I'd felt. It was as if I'd gone in search of Tyson and had unexpectedly crossed paths with long-lost loved ones, and we'd enjoyed a cup of coffee together.

I'd entered the session with an open mind, but I hadn't expected Mark, Chris, or Grandma Anne to show up. It had been twenty-nine years since I'd seen Grandma or Mark. If I'm honest, I have to admit I hadn't thought of them much for a long time. I hadn't thought of Chris much, either. I felt so blessed that they had stopped by for a visit to remind me of the love and connection we had once shared—that I now knew we *still* shared.

Something else struck me on the drive home; a poignant memory from 1993 when I was in my junior year of college, just a few years after Mark's passing. I had gone to see the movie *Philadelphia*, which stars Tom Hanks. It's about a Philadelphia lawyer, Andrew Beckett, who is fired for being homosexual.

Beckett (Hanks) eventually dies from complications of AIDS. At the very end of the film, home movies are played of Beckett as a child. They reminded me so much of home movies I had seen of Mark as a child. It made me feel so much love, compassion, and sadness for him.

Mark had often seemed so tormented and alone, even though there were many people who loved him. In those home movies, though, he was an innocent, happy kid, smiling and enjoying his family. Like Beckett, who also had been a happy, smiling kid, Mark had been broken down by life.

The similarities triggered an avalanche of emotion in me and I ran out of the theater, embarrassed by my tears. I hid behind a dumpster and cried for Mark. I cried longer and harder than I had in a long time.

I wished I'd recalled that memory during the session with Lisa, because I would have asked Mark if he had witnessed all this.

I would have asked if he had experienced the love I felt for him and if he had been comforted by the fact I understood his pain. I'm pretty sure he did.

One day, I'll ask him. For now, it was comforting to know he was at peace; that they *all* were.

62: ANOTHER SESSION WITH SONDY

I had another session with Sondy a few weeks later. I didn't really have a reason, and I didn't feel I needed one. I just missed Tyson and wanted to communicate with him.

I'd also grown curious about my shared past life with Tyson that Sondy had referred to before. The images I had pictured of me barefoot in overalls out in the country had really stuck with me. I was curious to know if Tyson could tell Sondy anything specific about that life.

"Can you ask him about the other life we shared?"

Sondy was silent for a few moments. Then she said, "You were really poor. I mean, like, Appalachia poor. I hate to stereotype, but I'm picturing you in overalls, barefoot. And you were a towhead. Tyson was a medium-sized dog."

Sondy hadn't given me any details about this other life during our first session, and I hadn't mentioned the image that had come to me. The closeness of her description was striking.

"You and Tyson spent a lot of time together in nature. It seems to be sometime close to the turn of the century, 1890 to 1910. You spent a lot of time together near a stream where there was a lot of fish and birds."

Again, this held the ring of truth. I'd always loved being out in nature.

"Your dad in that life was a very decent, hardworking man. He died very young, and you had to work very hard, taking care of your mom. Your mom was extremely protective of you, almost religiously so."

"Were my mom and dad people from my current life?"

"Your dad was your grandfather in this life."

I thought about my grandparents, and my paternal granddad certainly fit this description. He had fought in World War II and was a career police officer, retiring as Deputy Chief of Tampa, Florida. I've always had a ton of respect and admiration for him.

"My dad's dad?" I asked.

"No, I don't think so. Actually, I think he was your step-grandfather."

"Papa Stu?" I asked, referring to Grandma Anne's second husband.

"Bingo. That's actually what Tyson says."

This also blew my mind. Identifying Papa Stu as my step-grandfather was so specific, and it also felt right to me. "What about my mom in that life? Was she anyone in my current life?"

"It was Madison."

This came as a shock, but the more I thought about it, the more it made sense. We've always said that Madison is like an old lady, an old soul. She is also very protective of her loved ones, especially her animals.

When the session was over, I pondered what had been said and considered the value of the information. The accuracy of Sondy's description of my past life, as well as the loved ones from that life, was amazingly accurate. It also served as further validation that we live on after death and that we are spiritual beings having a human experience.

Still, I thought it best not to dwell on it too much. After all, I had a life to live, right then and there.

63: REIKI

After the mind-blowing sessions with Sondy and Lisa, I no longer doubted that there really was an afterlife. Both had told me that we all have a certain amount of psychic ability and that we can develop this. Looking back on my life, I can think of a handful of experiences I can only conclude were cases of divine intervention—and, in some cases, evidence of my own psychic ability.

Of course, these were extremely rare (at least my awareness of them was) and spread out over my forty-six years of life. I definitely had no conscious control over them. I'm confident that most people, if they're honest, can say the same thing.

I continued my daily practice of meditation, hoping to develop some of these abilities. I still experienced the loving, vibrant energy flowing through me, as well as the occasional sense that a loving spirit was standing right there next to me, but I could never say specifically what the sources of these sensations were.

Don't get me wrong, I'm not complaining. These energies were deeply comforting, and meditation always left me refreshed. Still, I was nowhere near being able to articulate the significance of these experiences other than the physical sensations, or what is called clairsentience. I hoped I would soon figure out what my metaphysical strengths were.

Around this time, I had coffee with my friend and police colleague Janet Harkness. Janet was an animal lover just like me, although her preference was cats over dogs. She had recently lost two kitties and had consulted with an animal communicator, achieving equally comforting results.

Janet had recently become a Reiki practitioner. I learned that Reiki is a Japanese form of energy healing that anyone can practice. She recommended that I look into it.

This seemed serendipitous to me because when I was searching around for online metaphysical courses, I found myself particularly drawn to energy healing. I decided to sign up for the same class Janet had taken, Reiki I with Anna Dorian of Vibrant Reiki in San Francisco. I attended the class in early December 2018.

During the weekend-long class, we learned that Reiki is spiritually guided life-force energy, and it is administered by "laying on hands." It was discovered by a Japanese doctor named Mikao Usui in 1922, although this same energy has been around for thousands of years.

Reiki is very simple, but it's very powerful—and, like Janet said, anyone can do it. I learned that the Reiki energy would be passed on to each of the students by Anna and two other Reiki Masters through an "attunement." This is like attaching a spiritual antenna to the student, henceforth giving them the ability to channel the energy.

This sounded awesome to me. But I'd be lying if I said I wasn't a bit skeptical, even in light of the incredible experiences I'd already had with Sondy and Lisa and the remarkably powerful energy I'd felt during my meditation sessions.

Was this energy really coming from a spiritual source, or was it simply heat from one's hands and nothing more than a placebo?

Before being attuned, we practiced hand positions and administering the energy. We also had thoughtful group discussions regarding Reiki and the powerful difference it can make in the world.

It was enjoyable and refreshing to spend the weekend with a group of people who simply wanted to help others. We all had this great intention in common, and it made it easy to connect with one another.

It had been explained that everyone's attunement experience was different; some people had intense experiences, while some people didn't experience much of anything.

When it came time for ours, I approached it with an open mind, but I hoped I would experience something that would eliminate my skepticism. I won't describe the actual process, but I will describe my experience.

As it started, we were instructed to close our eyes. I felt this beautiful heaviness, like I was being wrapped in love. I sensed that Tyson was there with me, and I instantly felt a surge of emotion that made me cry. Not a sob, just happy tears.

Throughout most of the process, which lasted about a half hour to forty-five minutes, I felt a loving presence standing close to me, to my left.

A couple of times, I peeked to see if one of the Reiki Masters were standing near me, and they were not. I was definitely feeling a spiritual presence.

Toward the end of the process, I no longer felt the presence on my left, but then I began to feel a similar presence on my right. The whole experience was quite beautiful, and I felt blessed.

After the attunement, we practiced administering the energy.

Everyone seemed to enjoy both receiving and giving, but I'd be lying if I said I felt anything. The whole vibe was incredibly warm and positive, but I couldn't discern any energy coming or going. This would change before long.

64: MISHA, MY WILLING TEST SUBJECT

After the class, I definitely believed that Reiki was real, but I wasn't convinced I would be able to effectively channel the energy. Misha's schedule was always hectic, but when I told her all she had to do was lay down and relax, she was more than willing to be my test subject—even though she was skeptical about Reiki.

The first treatment I gave her was right before bedtime. I worked on her for around a half hour. As I did, I practiced channeling the energy through my crown chakra, through my heart chakra, then through my hands. I began to feel energy, which I can best describe as mild electrical impulses, in my hands and fingers. Yet it was so mild that I questioned if I was only imagining it.

When the session was over, Misha was so relaxed that she went straight to bed and fell asleep. The next day, she reported that she'd slept so well she didn't move, not even an inch, the entire night. This was remarkable because Misha often had trouble quieting her mind at night, which caused difficulty getting a good night's rest.

Over the next couple of months, I performed Reiki on Misha two or three times a week, usually before bed. She consistently enjoyed the same great quality sleep. We soon found that it was also effective with hot flashes, which she'd recently started having. If I was with her when one struck, I'd simply hold her hand and start channeling Reiki. Within a matter of seconds, the hot flash would go away.

Over the next six months, I probably did this a good fifty times. There was only one instance when it took more than a few seconds to go away, but this was a particularly bad hot flash.

Misha had become a believer, often demanding that I put her on my schedule for a Reiki session.

Madison, on the other hand, wasn't particularly interested in receiving Reiki—probably because it required her to sit still. This, too, changed within a few months. If she was feeling sore from swimming or just generally under the weather, I'd give her Reiki during the half-hour drive to school. At first she would humor me, but soon she started asking for it.

With all of the practice on Misha and Madison, my ability to feel the energy grew significantly. This allowed me to know what body part to treat (if I felt a lot of energy flowing to a particular area), but also when to move to another position (if the energy had stopped flowing). It also gave me much more confidence, not only in my ability to give Reiki but also in the belief that this energy really existed.

My skeptical mind was still at work, but for me, the energy had become tangible. I couldn't see it—still can't!—but I sure could feel it.

65: HEARTLIGHT REPLAY

We have a gym in our garage, and I work out most days. While I do, I usually have music playing from one of my iTunes playlists.

Not long after my first Reiki class, I had the 80s playlist going, which happens to include *Heartlight* by Neil Diamond. No, it isn't a quintessential 80s song, but it came out in 1982, so it's in there.

Despite its sentimental connection to Tyson, I didn't actually download it until after he passed, but it is a powerful emotional trigger for me nonetheless.

I'd intentionally not listened to the song for a while. Aside from the fact it stirred up strong feelings of love for Tyson, it also made me feel emotionally raw.

I was still deep in the grieving process, and sadness still struck regularly, even without the obvious triggers. I didn't think it was healthy to add to this.

One day, I was working out, not thinking about much, when the song suddenly came on. In a matter of seconds, I fell from a calm state of enjoyment to a sobbing mess. I cried so hard I actually gasped for breath. I missed my Asshole of Love so much.

By the end of the song, I had regained my composure. I thought about how unwise it had been to add that song to a playlist, especially one I listened to regularly. It would only be a matter of time before it popped up again, whether I was ready for it or not. Despite this, I reveled in the love I was feeling for my lost friend.

The song ended, and I moved on to my next exercise, wondering what sonic piece of nostalgia would play next. To my astonishment, *Heartlight* began to play again.

Are you kidding me? I thought. *Do I have it set on repeat, to boot?*

I checked the file to see if it was set to repeat, but it wasn't. I checked to see if I had accidentally added the song to the playlist twice. Nope. The song was only in there once.

Thankfully, the replay didn't hit me like the first one did. My emotional breakdown had given me the catharsis I was apparently in need of. Still, it seemed odd. Unlikely. It certainly wouldn't have been the first time iTunes played a song twice within a short period of time, but I'd never had a song play twice in a row before.

I couldn't help but wonder if Tyson was reaching out to let me know he was with me. Later, I asked Lisa if this had been the case. She told me that it wasn't Tyson.

I'll admit that, in the meantime, I've had other songs play twice in a row for no apparent reason. Maybe it was just a software glitch after all. Whatever it was, it provided me with a little comfort at the time.

Since then, I've been able to listen to *Heartlight* without it tearing me up, although not too often because it still triggers a lot of strong emotions. It may have been written with *E.T.* in mind, but as far as I'm concerned, the song is about me and Tyson.

66: A BEER WITH FRIENDS

The experience with Lisa and the communication she had enabled with my relatives stayed with me. I began to wonder if I went back to see her again, would other loved ones come through? I decided it was worth trying, and I called Lisa to schedule another session.

As the session started, Lisa asked, "Did you have a childhood friend who died while you were in high school? It's the same friend who came through the first time you and I spoke by phone."

"No. I had acquaintances who died during high school, but no childhood friends."

"A childhood friend who died young, but not necessarily in high school. Blond hair? His name is something like Jerry."

I thought about Jeremy Stoner, a childhood friend of mine who died in a motorcycle accident in 2007. Although we'd grown up together, I lost touch with Jeremy after high school. We'd played baseball in the same league and were in the same den in Cub Scouts. In fact, his mom, Chris, was our den mother.

Jeremy and I were always friends and had a mutual respect, although we were never very close. It was a real gut punch when I found out he had passed, and I'd thought often of Chris and Jeremy's dad, Ken, over the years. They were a very close-knit family, so I knew Jeremy's loss was devastating.

I'd had recurring dreams about Chris and Ken ever since I learned about Jeremy, and in the summer of 2017, I'd finally reached out to Chris. Although I hadn't seen her in close to thirty years, we had a great visit, and I left with every intention of staying in touch.

"Jeremy?" I asked Lisa.

"Yes! Jeremy!"

It seemed this would be yet another remarkable session.

"He died in a car accident, right?"

"Well, he was on a motorcycle, but he collided with a car, yes. I recently reconnected with his mom. I've been having dreams about his parents ever since I found out about his passing."

"He says that he was sending those dreams to you to encourage you to reconnect with his parents. You reached out on Facebook, right?"

"Yes, that's right."

"He says that he never got to use Facebook, but he thinks it's neat. Did you play sports with him? He's showing me a red ball."

"Yes, we played in the same baseball league. Actually, we played every sport you could think of together at school during recess."

"He says that he admired your ability to run fast."

"I'm not fast anymore! But yes, I was very fast as a kid. Faster than most everyone in our elementary school."

"He had two daughters, right?"

"I believe so, yes."

"He is around them and his wife a lot. His wife has a new boyfriend, which he's very pleased about because he wants her to be happy. He also spends a lot of time at his childhood home with his parents. His childhood bedroom still has a lot of his belongings. He loves it when his daughters stay with his parents and sleep in his bedroom. It gives him comfort."

"I'll definitely pass this on to Chris and Ken," I said. "I know it will mean a lot to them."

"He is very much at peace, and he works with young kids on the other side, kind of like a day camp type of thing. Physically, he's in his twenties."

I could see Jeremy working with kids and being a role model, either here or on the other side.

"Did you have another childhood friend who died?" Lisa asked. "There is another person with him."

I thought for a second, but no one immediately came to mind.

"This person says he was a bully to you."

Lisa's words certainly narrowed things down. I'd had only a few bullies as a kid, but one of them had lived three houses away. Ben Roberts, who was a year and a half older than me, had been a lot like an older brother, complete with a fair amount of bullying. Despite this, we'd been pretty close friends until I was eleven, when Ben got into drugs. They destroyed his life.

Ben's parents had divorced when he was very young. To complicate things, his father hadn't been very present, which caused Ben to struggle quite a bit. Before the drugs, Ben was a smart person and a great athlete who might have become a professional baseball player if he hadn't lost his way. He had died of a methamphetamine overdose at the age of forty-three.

Talking to Lisa, I probably hadn't thought of Ben right away because, to my knowledge, he and Jeremy hadn't been close friends. It was surprising that they would be together on the other side.

"Ben?" I said.

"Yes, that's right. Ben. Did he die of a drug overdose? He's showing me a hypodermic needle."

"Yes, he did. I'm pretty sure it was methamphetamine."

"He wants his family to know that the overdose was an accident, that he didn't commit suicide."

I promised I would pass the information on to Dindy Roberts, Ben's mom. "Can you tell him that although his bullying was hurtful, most of the time I thought of him as a big brother?"

Lisa laughed. "He's being cocky. He says you *were* his little brother, so of course he bullied you!"

"Yeah, I guess. That certainly is something he would say!"

"He thinks it's very cool that you get to carry a gun at work."

"That's funny. I remember shooting pellet guns with him when we were young."

"He says that he spends a lot of time at his childhood home with his mom. She finds comfort in spending time in his bedroom. He wants his family to know that he is at peace and healthy, physically in his twenties. Also, he recognizes that he could have lived a much more happy and productive life. He wants to reincarnate sooner than later."

I was happy to hear this. Like I said, I hadn't had a lot of contact with Ben after the age of eleven, but I knew he had a lot of problems. He also had potential; probably more than anyone from my childhood.

With a healthier mindset, he could have led an enormously successful life.

Lisa echoed this sentiment when she said, "He is a young soul, but he's very smart."

"Yes, he sure was. Up until he got into drugs, school came very easy to him. He was an A student and a very gifted athlete."

"He says that he had a girlfriend before he died, but that she wasn't right for him." At this point, Lisa paused for a moment. "They are both still here, Jeremy and Ben, and I'm having a hard time deciphering between their energies." She paused again before continuing. "Jeremy says that he still loves motorcycles, and he often rides with you. Do you ride motorcycles?"

"Yes, I do. I'm a motorcycle officer at work, and I also have a bike of my own, so I ride quite a bit."

"He rides with you both for enjoyment and to protect you. He's one of your spiritual guides. He especially likes to ride with you when you ride through your old childhood neighborhood."

Just a couple of weeks prior, I had taken a nostalgic ride through the old neighborhood. By now, I no longer felt surprised that Lisa could know these things.

"Yes!" I said. "I rode through the old neighborhood—"

"He says that you interrupted him," Lisa said, cutting me off. Then she started laughing. "Did you guys have a habit of interrupting each other? He says that you rode through the neighborhood a couple of weeks ago, and that he was with you."

This made me laugh too because it sounded just like Jeremy. He would always grow impatient if you interrupted him, and he wasn't afraid to call you on it.

Lisa started to speak again, then stopped. She told me again that she was having difficulty deciphering between Jeremy and Ben. As I took a moment to appreciate the magnitude of what I was experiencing, I felt nothing but love for these friends.

"Can you tell them that I love them?" I said.

"Oh, they know you do," Lisa said. She paused again, then

continued. "Jeremy wanted to be a firefighter. He always wanted to wear a uniform."

"I don't know if he did or not. I know he worked for the water district."

"Jeremy and Ben are together a lot on the other side. There are other deceased friends from your old neighborhood there as well. Ben spends a lot of time just kicking back."

There were two other young men from our neighborhood who had passed, Dale Yearian in 1992 and James Baca in 2017, so this made sense. James and Ben had been fairly close, especially later. Ben had always been fond of kicking back and relaxing, so this fit as well.

"Jeremy says that he really loved the outdoors. He loved camping and that sort of thing, but he didn't like hunting because he loved animals."

This seemed a little off to me. I had thought Jeremy was fond of hunting and fishing. This brought my mind back to a meditation session from a few weeks prior. During that meditation, I saw images of the wooded park area behind Ben's childhood home. More specifically, I saw a metal gate and an old shed from a park staff residence. It occurred to me that maybe Ben, not Jeremy, had sent me these images. I asked Lisa to ask him.

"He says the images didn't come from him," Lisa explained, "but he recognizes that a spiritual gate has opened for you, and it's important that you walk through. He also says that he could relate to you better after your parents divorced."

While Ben and I hadn't grown closer after my parents' divorce, it still made sense. Up until the divorce, most everyone believed we had an idyllic family. Given his dad's absence, I'm sure Ben was envious and maybe even resentful. Watching me experience some of the same pain he'd gone through would likely have given him a sense of kinship.

"He wishes that his mom had moved out of their home after the divorce because all of the memories of their family before the divorce were painful for him."

This was something I could absolutely relate to. When Dad left, our house became a constant reminder of what had been lost. Still, when Mom sold it a few years later, I was very sad. I'm sure Ben would have been too.

"He left," Lisa said abruptly with a giggle.

I was surprised. "Just like that?"

"Yep. He said, 'I'm out' and left. I think maybe he got too tired from connecting. They have to lower their vibration to connect with us, and it takes a lot out of them."

This cracked me up. An abrupt departure like this without a cordial goodbye sounded just like Ben. Still, I appreciated that he had made the effort to connect.

"Jeremy is still here, though," Lisa said. "He wants his loved ones to move on and find peace regarding him. He wants them to always remember him, but he doesn't want them to suffer, especially his mom. Her pain actually drags him down."

It came as no surprise that Jeremy would be concerned about his mom. To this day, Chris still struggles with losing him. It isn't easy on Ken, either. But it's particularly hard on Chris. I hoped hearing Jeremy wanted her to find peace would help her to heal.

"I'll make a point to pass this on to them," I promised.

Then Lisa shifted gears. "Were you recently working on something creative?"

When I hear the word "creative," my mind goes straight to movies and screenplays. It had been a couple of years since I had put any significant effort into a movie. "Nothing in particular, not that I can think of."

"Hmmm. Like maybe some kind of decorating?"

Since our move to Pleasanton, I'd been slowly but surely building a man cave in our garage. It had an 80s theme, and by the time it was finished would feature between twenty and thirty 11x17 movie posters, a ton of 80s arcade games, neon lights, a ping pong table, a dartboard, and a bar. A couple of weeks earlier, I'd added several new posters.

I mentioned this to Lisa and asked if that sounded like what she was referring to.

"Yep, that's it!" she said. "He was there with you. He thinks your man cave is very cool."

This made me smile. "He can hang out there anytime."

"He wants to know if you play pool. He says he could whoop you."

Now, this definitely sounded like Jeremy. It brought back memories from high school, like the time he challenged me to a tennis match and I beat him. His parents had owned a pool table for decades, so he'd had lots of practice.

"I'm sure he *could* whoop me," I admitted. "But I'll bet I could whoop him at ping pong!"

Lisa laughed at the good-natured ribbing. Then Jeremy shifted to a more complimentary tone.

"He's proud of the life you are living, and he loves that you have a daughter who you can teach about the role of a man and a dad."

These words meant a lot to me. Jeremy had never been one to throw out compliments halfheartedly. I wished that I could hug him.

"He really admires the way you always stay focused on things to achieve your goals," Lisa added.

I felt myself blush. This comment meant so much to me. It was also very accurate. Every significant accomplishment I've achieved in my life required perseverance and discipline. I wouldn't call myself an overachiever, but I've worked hard. Very little has come easy to me. It was pretty cool to hear this from a respected friend, especially one with a view from the "other side."

What really struck me about my interaction with Jeremy was the level of connection we had. If someone had asked me how close we had been before the session with Lisa, I would have said that we grew up together, but that we weren't very close. Yet the level of mutual love, respect, and understanding communicated through Lisa made it clear I had underestimated the connection Jeremy and I had.

"I really wish we had been closer," I said.

"He says that his ego got in the way," Lisa replied.

Although we'd spent time together on the ball field and in Cub Scouts, Jeremy had been one of the "cool kids," and I wasn't. He always had girlfriends. I *never* did. I wasn't what anyone would have called a nerd, but I definitely wasn't part of the "in" crowd.

"I guess that makes sense," I said. "He was always decent to me, though. I'm sure we'll have another chance at some point."

"Absolutely, you will," Lisa agreed. "Do you have anything else you would like to say to Jeremy?"

I knew there was probably something I would think of later, but nothing came to mind.

"No," I said, "I don't think so. Just please thank him for making the effort to visit. It means a lot to me."

Lisa thanked Jeremy, and the session ended. On the drive home, I replayed the session in my head. Like the session with Mark, Chris, Grandma Anne, and Tyson, the feeling of connection with Jeremy and Ben was what resonated the most. I felt as if I'd just had a get-together with two old friends for beers. Naturally, my skeptical mind considered if Lisa could have somehow learned of my connection to Jeremy and Ben. In the end, the only thing that made logical sense was that she had really communicated with them.

I wanted to smack myself when I realized later that I had completely overlooked an obvious irony during the session. A couple of months prior, just before Christmas, I'd paid visits to Jeremy's parents, Chris and Ken, and to Ben's mom, Dindy. I brought them copies of two books I thought might bring them some peace.

The first book, *Many Lives, Many Masters* by Brian Weiss, M.D., tells the true story of a psychiatrist who, after two years of unsuccessfully attempting to alleviate a patient's many phobias, decides to try hypnotic regression therapy to determine the experiential causes of the phobias. Instead of regressing to different points in her life, the patient regresses to points in *past* lives.

The second book, *Talking to Heaven* by James Van Praagh, tells the story of Van Praagh's journey toward becoming a spiritual medium and shares many examples of communication with the other side.

I believed that even if they were skeptical, Chris, Ken, and Dindy would be heartened by the accounts shared within the pages of the books. The irony of Jeremy and Ben coming through after such a recent outreach to their parents was beyond coincidental. I thought hard and asked myself if I had ever mentioned anything about Jeremy and Ben to Lisa. I hadn't.

I thought about the recurring dreams I'd had about Chris and Ken, and how I had felt compelled to reach out to them. I also considered my decision to bring the books to them, and to Dindy. The best way to describe it was that I had felt guided.

Could all of this be a crazy coincidence? Possibly. But if I said I believed that was all there was to it, I'd be lying through my teeth.

67: BEING THE MESSENGER

I hadn't yet had my session with Jeremy and Ben when I brought the books to Chris, Ken, and Dindy. While Chris and Dindy were open-minded when I shared with them the details of having communicated with Uncle Mark, Aunt Chris, and Grandma Anne, Ken wasn't. I couldn't blame him. It was something I probably wouldn't have believed myself. Telling them that I had communicated with their sons was another thing entirely.

My biggest concern was that it might cause them pain. That was the last thing I wanted. But I truly believed that Jeremy and Ben wanted to bring their parents peace. I felt it was my duty to pass along their messages.

I sat down with Chris and Ken first. When I told them that Jeremy had come through during my session, Chris was intrigued but not surprised. Ken, though cordial, seemed skeptical. I was thankful that they were both willing to hear me out.

I told them everything Jeremy had communicated through Lisa. They seemed pleased with the positive messages meant for me, and I hoped they found the accuracy compelling. The messages meant for them were received warmly, although they indicated that while some of the messages were accurate, others were not.

They seemed comforted that Jeremy wanted his wife to be happy and to move on. They confirmed that she had started dating someone. They were happy for her. When I told them Jeremy wanted all of his loved ones to be at peace with his passing, I emphasized that he was particularly concerned about Chris. They seemed to take this to heart, especially Chris. She smiled with loving angst and said, "I know. It's hard."

They confirmed that Jeremy had been quite good at pool, which I'd already guessed as he'd grown up with a pool table at home. But I was surprised by Chris's response when I told her that Jeremy said many of his childhood belongings were still at their home, and that he was comforted when his daughters slept in his childhood bedroom.

She told me that when he moved from home, Jeremy had taken most of his childhood belongings with him, but that she still had quite a few gifts he'd given her during his childhood. She said that many of these gifts, like stuffed animals, could be mistaken for childhood belongings.

Chris also informed me that although Jeremy's daughters did sometimes spend the night, they usually slept on the large couch in their entertainment room—not in Jeremy's old bedroom.

When I brought up Lisa's statement about Jeremy having been an animal lover and not fond of hunting, Ken humorously corrected me. "He may have loved animals," Ken said, "but he sure was good at killing them." As I had accurately recalled during the session with Lisa, his parents confirmed that Jeremy had been an avid fisherman and hunter since childhood.

I told them that Jeremy said he'd always wanted to be a firefighter. They could neither confirm nor deny this.

"That could be," Chris said. "He wanted to be a lot of things."

It seemed Lisa hadn't been as accurate with Jeremy's communications as she had been with my family members. I wondered if maybe she had confused Ben's messages for Jeremy's. After all, she did say she was having trouble differentiating between them.

I asked Chris and Ken if they had ever known Ben Roberts. They knew who he was but told me he hadn't been a friend of Jeremy's. In fact, Chris was fairly certain Jeremy hadn't cared for Ben. Ken pointed out that he had worked with Ben's dad back in the 1970s, and that although the two families had socialized at company parties, as far as he knew that was the extent of Jeremy's connection with Ben.

I wondered if they found it interesting when I told them that Ben and Jeremy were often together on the other side, along with other people from the neighborhood who had passed.

Overall, my visit with Chris and Ken was a good one. Seeing them was and is still a great pleasure, and the messages I passed along seemed to be well received. Still, I worried that the experience was painful for them. I was especially concerned that the inaccurate information would make them less open to the overall message. I hoped that once they had time to process the information it would bring them peace.

My visit with Dindy Roberts, Ben's mom, was more strained. I had already called ahead and told her that Ben had come through in my second session with Lisa and that I wanted to give her his messages. Straight off the bat, she was wary of my visit, and although she was cordial, she wasn't particularly friendly.

I knew she appreciated the books I'd given her and that she was fascinated with the information I'd shared about my first session with Lisa, but she seemed very uneasy about hearing from Ben. I understood that the new information could disrupt whatever perspectives and coping mechanisms she had employed to get through Ben's death, so I empathized with her. Still, I believed it was my duty to give her Ben's messages.

As with Jeremy's parents, I told Dindy everything Ben had communicated. Though mostly accurate, there were some discrepancies and information that left Dindy a bit skeptical. For example, when I told her what Lisa had said about Ben overdosing with a hypodermic needle, Dindy told me Ben had smoked the methamphetamine but never injected it. Regardless, it still made sense to me that Ben would convey the image of a needle because it seemed the easiest way to get across "drug overdose."

Next, when I shared what Ben had communicated about Dindy being comforted by spending time in his old bedroom, she strongly disagreed. Ben had died in that room, and to her, it was a terrible place of sadness. Then she told me something I didn't know: Ben's girlfriend had moved in with Dindy after his death and now occupied Ben's old bedroom.

When I told her that Ben said he hadn't been terribly into this woman, and that their relationship wasn't one for the long haul, Dindy strongly agreed.

I wondered if it was possible that some of the information Lisa had attributed to Jeremy could have actually been coming from Ben. I asked Dindy some questions that I hoped would help me clarify. I asked her if Ben had been an animal lover, and Dindy emphatically confirmed this. She added that Ben believed animals should be protected, and he wasn't fond of hunting. She also confirmed that he'd enjoyed the outdoors.

I asked her if Ben had wanted to become a firefighter, and she replied with a resounding "Yes!" Being a firefighter had always been a dream of Ben's, she said, and Dindy had always believed he'd have made a great one if not for his drug issues.

That sealed it, as far as I was concerned. Lisa had simply mistaken Ben's messages for Jeremy's. I hoped such specific information was compelling for Dindy and that it would help open her heart and mind to Ben's other messages. I also looked forward to explaining the confusion to Chris and Ken.

I told Dindy what Lisa had said about Ben being very smart. Dindy confirmed that school had always come easily to him and that he had consistently tested within the top ten percent of students. I knew he was smart, but I didn't know he'd tested so high. Dindy spoke of this with a mix of pride and regret. I shared these feelings, but the last thing I wanted was for Dindy to walk away from our meeting feeling sad and regretful.

I told her that Ben wanted her to know he was at peace and healthy, and that he wanted her and the rest of the family to be equally at peace. I added that Ben hoped to reincarnate sooner than later and that he intended to live up to his potential in his next life. This seemed to brighten her mood, if only a bit.

When I told her that the communication with Ben had ended with an abrupt "I'm out," she seemed amused. She reminisced about Ben's short attention span, and that this sort of abrupt departure from a task was pretty typical of him. I was glad the last thing I told her about the session seemed to be affirming and positive.

Afterward, I reflected on our visit. I honestly couldn't tell if what I shared had been a comfort to her or not. To me, the inaccuracies were so greatly outweighed by the accuracies that the messages should have been credible to Dindy, Chris, and Ken.

Considering that Jeremy and Ben were so clear about being at peace and wanting the same for their loved ones, I hoped their parents would be comforted. Of course, I had the advantage of actually being in the session with Lisa and experiencing it firsthand. If I'd heard the information secondhand, I probably would have been skeptical myself—and skepticism has a way of squashing comfort.

With that in mind, I strongly encouraged Chris, Ken, and Dindy to reach out to Lisa for a session of their own. Although my encouragements haven't yet moved them to take that step, I hope they someday will.

68: REIKI II

Ever since my first class, I'd made a daily effort to give myself Reiki during my meditations. I also continued to give Reiki to Misha regularly. I occasionally offered it to friends, but I was still trying to build my confidence.

Right around the time I spoke to Jeremy's and Ben's parents, I attended the second level of Reiki training. Once again, my teacher was Anna Dorian. I was excited about this training because it would give me, the student, the ability to send Reiki through time and space.

This meant I would not only be given the ability to send it from a distance but to different times. For example, I could send Reiki to myself during the time of my parents' divorce.

I know the whole concept sounds very far-fetched. I was skeptical myself. But if I had legitimately communicated with deceased friends and family members, and if I had been able to eliminate Misha's hot flashes and help her sleep better by channeling healing energy through my hands—and I believed that in both cases I had—was it a huge leap to think the same healing energy could be channeled from a distance? After all, it wasn't coming from me. I was only channeling it. Why would energy coming from the spiritual realm be limited to what I could touch?

The class was enjoyable, much like the first one I'd taken. Not only were we the students prepared to receive the distance and time attunements, but we also practiced giving each other Reiki.

I experienced an intensely powerful affirmation when my first partner, Karen, was working on me. My eyes were closed, and she'd been working on my shoulders for a while. Suddenly, I felt someone start to work on my knees at the same time. This surprised me because we were supposed to be working in groups of two, but I figured maybe Anna had joined us. When I opened my eyes, I was shocked to see Karen working on my knees. There was no one working on my shoulders, yet I could feel someone's hands on them. I told Anna what I was experiencing, and she said she'd seen this phenomenon many times before.

When it was time for me to receive the attunements to give me the ability to send Reiki through time and space, I wondered if the experience would be as powerful as my first attunement. It wasn't. While I could briefly feel the presence of spirits close to me, the sensation wasn't nearly as strong as it had been with the first level. I also didn't experience the surge of powerful emotions that had accompanied my first attunement. I didn't let this worry me. I knew the experience was different for everyone.

After the class, I was eager to start sending Reiki to as many people as I could. Not only did I want to help others, but I also needed the practice. Being able to send from a distance allowed me to do so from the comfort of our home on a daily basis, and coordinating schedules was a non-issue since I was the only one who needed to be present.

One of the first people I sent to was my brother, Chason, who'd been nursing a mild case of peroneal tendinitis in his right foot. He'd been prescribed orthotic inserts a few days before, and things had improved some, but he was still in a fair amount of pain. He was open to receiving Reiki, although he wasn't necessarily a believer. I think he was just tired of hurting, so he was willing to try anything.

I advised him I would soon begin sending the energy, and I proceeded to do so for about twenty minutes. When I was done, I texted him to let him know. He enthusiastically reported being able to feel vibrations in his feet, and he was able to pinpoint precisely when I had stopped because the vibrations had stopped.

Most importantly, his feet felt significantly better than they had before the session. Even with the success I'd had giving Reiki to Misha, I'd be lying if I said that I was totally convinced. The cynic in me wanted to attribute Chason's observations and improvement to the placebo effect, but it was very affirming nonetheless. Chason's foot only got better from there.

My childhood friend Jim Gomez, who lived in Ohio, had recently told me about his stepdaughter Iva's chronic migraine issues. They had been plaguing her for a couple of years, and in that time Iva had sought medical help and tried a number of interventions like changing her diet, exercising, and CBD oil. Nothing worked. She even dropped out of college because the headaches were causing her to miss too many classes.

I offered to send Reiki to Iva if she was open to it. She responded with, "Sure, that's so sweet," which told me she was touched by the gesture but clearly didn't take it seriously. The same day I sent to Chason, I began sending to Iva. To our collective astonishment, her migraines, which had been occurring daily, miraculously stopped.

I sent her Reiki for another two weeks before checking in again. She reported that aside from one minor migraine that had lasted ten minutes, she hadn't had another headache. As I write this, it's been ten months and Iva is still migraine-free.

Iva's mom, Maggie, was so blown away that she asked me to send Reiki for her right arm. She'd been dealing with chronic tendinitis in her right elbow and wrist for a couple of weeks. I worked on her for about a half hour. When I called to let her know I'd finished, Maggie told me she could tell when I started because her arm had suddenly become very warm. The best part was that the pain was gone.

Maggie owned a fence company and performed a lot of manual labor, so I figured tendinitis and the like were inevitable, but I was amazed when she told me several months later that the pain in her arm had not returned.

Soon, my confidence had improved to the point where I was offering people Reiki every day, both in-person and from a distance. Although police officers tend to be a notoriously skeptical group, I've made believers out of a number of my colleagues.

One morning at the station, I crossed paths in the hallway with our detective sergeant, Giorgio Chavez, and asked him how he was doing. He said he had a horrible headache. When I offered him Reiki, he said, "Hey, man, I'll try anything."

I told him I'd come down to the detective unit in a few minutes. When I got there, it was clear he'd told the other detectives I'd be performing some woo-woo energy healing, because they started cracking jokes. They were good-natured jokes, but jokes nonetheless. One of the detectives even started playing meditation music.

I went to work on Giorgio and very quickly felt a huge amount of energy flowing. Within a couple of minutes, he said, "This is crazy, but I can feel the pain draining from my head."

I worked on him for a total of five minutes before the pain left altogether. Later, he told me he'd been pain-free for the remainder of the day.

Not long after that, I was working at my desk in the Special

Enforcement unit when I overheard an officer tell my sergeant that she'd strained her wrist a couple of days before and it had been hurting ever since. After my sergeant encouraged her to give it a try, she skeptically accepted my offer of Reiki.

I didn't feel much as I began to work on her, but soon the energy began to flow nicely. After about five minutes, I stopped and said, "Try that out."

She moved her wrist around, feeling for any changes, then burst out with an entertaining expletive: "What the *hell?*" Only she didn't actually say "hell."

The pain was gone. When I followed up with her the next day, she said the pain was still gone.

This became something of a frequent occurrence at work. In another instance, one of my fellow officers, Rayna Cawley, asked me if I had any ibuprofen. She had a cold and was suffering from a pretty powerful headache.

I told her that yes, I had ibuprofen, but would she be willing to try Reiki first?

"Sure," she replied with a shrug.

I pressed my hands gently against her temples. As I began to work on her, she described feeling electricity in her hands. "It's creepy!" she exclaimed, sounding amazed. Not surprisingly, her headache disappeared within minutes and did not return.

I am a member of the peer support team for our police and fire departments. We offer emotional support to police officers, firefighters, lifeguards, and dispatchers who are struggling with personal and professional stressors. During one peer support team meeting, I was telling everyone about my experiences with Reiki.

As a joke, I put my hand on my friend Pete DeQuincy's leg seductively. By way of experiment, I focused on sending him Reiki when I touched him. The next time I saw him a couple of days later, he told me that for about an hour after the meeting ended, he could feel energy flowing into his leg.

Before I knew it, Reiki had become a part of who I was, and I was finding daily fulfillment in helping people wherever I could. One afternoon, I was talking on the phone with my old boss and friend, Dan Macdonald. When he mentioned in passing that his big right toe had been hurting for a while, I told him about Reiki and that I could send it to him from a distance.

Not surprisingly, he was skeptical. As our conversation continued on to other subjects, unbeknownst to Dan, I began sending him Reiki. After about twenty minutes of doing this while we spoke, I informed him I'd been working on him for a bit, and I asked him to try walking on it.

A few seconds later, Dan blurted out, "That's weird!" His toe was no longer hurting.

I was getting a haircut from my longtime barber, Kevin Nguyen, and he told me that his lower back had been hurting for a couple of weeks. Later that day, I sent Reiki to him at two different times. By that afternoon, he reported that he was feeling much better. The next day, he asked me to send it one more time, which I did. The pain went away completely. The next time I came in for a haircut, Kevin told me the pain had not returned. Aside from my sending him Reiki, he hadn't sought out any other back treatments.

During a chiropractic visit, I told my doctor about the success I was having with Reiki, including the fact I could send it from a distance. I asked him if he had any aches or pains he needed help with, and he said that his upper trapezius and shoulders had been tight all day.

As a demonstration, I sent Reiki to his shoulders from across the treatment room. His eyes widened like saucers when he told me that his shoulders had suddenly gone numb. After the treatment, the tightness subsided.

Another time, I was on patrol in a park in Oakland when I crossed paths with park volunteer Jackie Palacios and her dog, Mickey. She told me Mickey had recently been experiencing a lot of discomfort in his hips, which made hiking difficult for him.

Jackie had just picked up some medication for Mickey from the vet. Being the dog lover I am, I wanted to help. Plus, my hands were buzzing with energy. I figured Reiki might do him some good. When I offered to work on Mickey, Jackie told me she'd been receiving treatments from a Reiki practitioner for a long time and it was a huge help. She was happy to let me give it a shot with Mickey.

I only worked on Mickey for a few minutes, but the energy was flowing so strong that I knew it had to be helping.

"Oh, he likes that!" Jackie said.

When I was done, Mickey stood and hopped into the back of Jackie's van with an agility she said she hadn't seen for a while. It did my heart a lot of good to see the little guy feeling better.

About a week later, Jackie texted me to thank me for the treatment and to report that Mickey was back to his energetic, loud self ever since. Even more amazingly, she hadn't had to give him any of the vet's medication.

I was in my favorite coffee shop, Valley Java in Castro Valley, when I overheard a customer talking to the owner about his cancer treatment. After their conversation was over, I approached the customer, a wonderful guy named Tony, and introduced myself. I told him a little about Reiki and offered to start sending it to him if he was open to it. He was.

Over the next few months, I sent to Tony several times per week, always letting him know after I finished. He always responded with a good-natured thanks and an update on his progress. I also frequently saw him at the coffee shop, and I was always impressed by how warm and positive he was, despite his battle. It wasn't long before Tony made my day by telling that me he was cancer-free. I'll never know how much the Reiki contributed to his healing, but I was honored to have been able to help, even if just a little.

These are just some examples of the incredible experiences I've had over the past year. It seems that rarely a day passes when I don't add another example to the list. I'm thankful every day to be able to offer the gift of Reiki. What's truly remarkable is that my ability to do so isn't special at all. Literally anyone who wants to do it, can! It doesn't take any special psychic gift. All it takes is the desire to help others.

69: TYSON, MY SPIRIT GUIDE

During my second Reiki class with Anna Dorian, she offered to perform a spiritual reading for me. I'd struggled with guided meditations, and she believed she could find out why. I was eager to let her have a crack.

After the reading, she told me that I had lived a past life during either the Greek or Roman times and that I had been a spiritual healer and teacher. According to her, I had been considered a heretic and murdered for my beliefs. She told me I still had lingering reservations about metaphysical beliefs because of that experience. Then she assured me that it was perfectly safe to embrace those beliefs now, as this was the safest time in history to do so.

To be perfectly honest, this did not resonate with me, but I did believe it was possible.

Next, Anna told me that Tyson was my spiritual guide and that he was helping me with my progression with Reiki. This, of course, *did* resonate.

"Have you thought of writing a book about your story, and about Tyson?" she asked.

Hearing this was like getting smacked in the head with love. I had been considering the idea of writing a book about Tyson's life and death for several months, but it was just an idea. I figured that if Tyson ever came back to us, this would be the ultimate conclusion to the story, so I had just decided to wait and see what happened. I hadn't mentioned the idea to anyone but Misha and maybe my dad, so Anna had no way of knowing about it.

"Yes, actually, I have," I said. "I was thinking that Tyson's return would make a great ending."

"Well," Anna said, "Tyson says that it is a really big deal that you write this book. He also said that your identity as a cop will help you connect with a wider, less woo-woo audience."

"Hmmm, interesting. It'll either do that, or it'll make people hate it before they even read it!" I said jokingly.

"Actually, this really seems like a big deal. So much so that I wouldn't be surprised if this book was one of your major life missions."

The idea of our little story getting out there and touching other people gave me a shot of emotion that brought tears to my eyes. I loved the idea of my boy being immortalized in a book that allowed others to benefit from his beautiful life.

After the session, I pondered the book and what its message would be. I knew I wanted to write about what a unique, crazy little dog Tyson was, but I wasn't sure how I wanted to present the impact of his death. I wanted to share the spiritual growth I had experienced, but it seemed like that was a story very much still in development. It also seemed like the story would be incomplete without Tyson's return. Why would I want to write an incomplete book?

The whole thing seemed daunting. I knew I would write it, and I believed that it could in fact be one of my life's missions. I just wasn't sure if now was the right time. As it turned out, the right time was coming.

70: A QUICK VISIT TO SEDONA

Every spring since 2011, Misha and I make an annual trip to Arizona for Major League Baseball's spring training. I've been a San Francisco Giants fan most of my life, and it's something I look forward to every year. An added bonus is that my sister, Andrea, and her family live in the area, as well as my mom.

Watching baseball in the perfect Arizona spring climate was therapeutic as usual, and our visit with Andrea and her family was great as always. Unfortunately, our visit with Mom was reminiscent of the days after the divorce—complete with Mom hurling vicious insults and hate speech without discretion.

Unfortunately, Mom's health had been bad for some time, largely due to many years of smoking. She repeatedly injured herself by tripping and falling because she refused to use her walker. Her diet was often poor because she had trouble cooking for herself. She really needed help managing her life, and Andrea had been doing her best to care for her for years. But rather than see the reality of the situation, Mom resented Andrea and accused her of trying to control her life.

When Mom began badmouthing Andrea and saying one of my least favorite Momisms—"She's making me feel like a piece of shit!"—I unwisely remarked, "Seriously, Mom? You're still saying that after all these years?"

Not surprisingly, Mom turned her anger on me. I did my best to deflect her attacks with humor, but it didn't help. It just pissed her off more. She even went after Misha at one point. Naturally, Dad received a few daggers of his own. After all, he *was* the root of all Mom's misery!

The whole visit with Mom only lasted around thirty minutes, at which point she mercifully (although without merciful intention) ordered us to leave.

I had endured these types of interactions with Mom almost daily during the first couple of years after the divorce, but it had been a while since our last one. I was totally disgusted, and I wouldn't have admitted it at the time, but I was also hurt. It was hard to believe that after all these years, Mom still had so much venom in her and such willingness to unleash it on those she loved.

Misha was in shock. She'd seen Mom be nasty before, but this display was on a level that was new to her. I would have preferred that Misha not have to experience it, but I was also comforted by the fact she now had a greater understanding of the hell I went through as a kid.

As we drove away, I dismissed the whole visit as "nothing new" and decided that I would not be having any contact with Mom for a long, long time.

The next day, we took a day trip to Sedona, which is about a two-hour drive north of Phoenix. It's a beautiful place with remarkable red-rock formations, and it's also a mecca for metaphysical spiritual exploration and practice. We had been there a number of times in the past, but not before my recent spiritual growth, so this trip would be a whole new experience.

As we pulled into town, I was drawn to a metaphysical store I'd noticed during our previous visits. The Center for the New Age was inside a purple building with orange trim and had a sign that read *Vortex Information*.

We'd made fun of this sign in the past, but now things were different. Although I had never had any desire to check it out before, I was now seeing it from a much different point of view.

At this point in my life, I was meditating daily and had been since Tyson's passing. Not only was I enjoying the physical and mental benefits, but I was also trying to develop my intuitive ability. But except for occasionally being able to sense the presence of spirit, this ability didn't seem to be progressing, and I was bewildered as to why. I wondered if I was trying too hard. My abilities with Reiki were progressing nicely, and maybe that was enough.

Misha and I went inside and looked around. I discovered that their gem and stone collection alone was worth checking out, but they also had several intuitives and spiritual mediums who practiced out of the facility. I began reading about them.

As I did, one of them, Aumara, walked by and checked in with the receptionist. My gut told me to make an appointment with her if it was possible. Sure enough, she had a slot open in just a few minutes.

When I sat down with Aumara, she told me to be careful not to tell her anything about myself, as she didn't want to be clouded by bias. This, of course, was nothing new to me. Lisa Silverman had adamantly told me the same thing. After "scanning" each of my chakras (spiritual energy centers), Aumara told me some things that were both helpful and comforting.

First, she told me that I was a protector and that I had been a protector several times before in previous lives. "Protectors are often police officers, firefighters, and healers," she said. This seemed to validate my career choice, as well as my pursuit of Reiki.

Next, she told me she sensed pain in my ear. This meant that I either had an ear issue or was in the process of developing my intuitive abilities, she said.

I told her I didn't have ear pain but that I'd been trying rather unsuccessfully to develop intuitively. She disagreed with me and said I was developing nicely. I told her about my pursuit of Reiki and my ability to perceive the energy, and she pointed out that this was a strong sign of development.

I shared with her my frustration at my lack of development in other intuitive areas, specifically clairvoyance and clairaudience. Aumara told me not to be concerned about this but rather to focus on my ability with energy healing. This was comforting to hear because it validated the idea that I should quit trying so hard and just focus on what had already been coming naturally. I felt like I could now cut myself some slack and enjoy the process more.

What Aumara said next surprised me. She said that I was healing from an issue with my mother. This didn't really jibe with what I was feeling. I'd dismissed our last visit with Mom as "nothing new," and aside from Misha and I cracking a few jokes about how awful she'd been, I hadn't thought much about her since.

Still, when Aumara pointed this out, I knew she was right. I was wounded pretty good. Right or wrong, at that moment my intent to cut off relations with Mom for the foreseeable future was reinforced.

I told Aumara about Tyson. She said that he remained close to me, which of course was no surprise.

Since my conversation with Anna about writing a book, I'd been trying to get started but had gotten nowhere. By this point, I had decided to wait until Tyson reincarnated.

As Misha put it, "Don't worry about it! If the Bobo wants the book written bad enough, he'll just have to do his part and come back to us."

I told Aumara about the book and my plan to wait until Tyson's return, to which she quickly replied, "No, that will be book two."

This jolted me. Her words were spoken with a certainty that seemed to indicate Tyson would surely be coming back. Both Lisa and Sondy had said Tyson wasn't sure if and when he would come back, so this was exciting to hear.

When I told Aumara that a book without Tyson's return didn't seem like a very compelling approach, she disagreed. There was plenty of story already there to tell, she said, and despite my own feelings of doubt, her conviction was hard to dismiss. I decided at that moment to write the book, despite my doubts.

When the session was over, I felt rejuvenated. I had a whole lot of work ahead of me, both with the book and with Reiki, but I was no longer worried about the outcome. It seemed like my life was being driven by goodness, and that was a wonderful feeling.

Misha smiled when I rendezvoused with her for lunch. "It must have been a good session," she remarked. "You're glowing!"

71: FORGIVE YOUR MOTHER

My anger toward Mom festered after the trip to Arizona. I kept replaying her display of wrath in my head, and it brought back a lot of memories and feelings from those miserable years after the divorce. I had long ago forgiven her for those times, but it was hard not to get triggered when she acted the same hateful way about something else.

Having Misha there to witness it was a comfort, but it also made it worse because it hurt her, too. She said it made her sad, not just for me and Mom, but also for what I had gone through years ago. I marveled at how little Mom had grown over the years; how she still held the same misplaced grudges and resentments, and how they were still holding her in a self-made emotional prison.

On the one hand, I truly felt sorry for her because she is a good person who I believe could have found happiness. On the other hand, it infuriated me because she still hadn't come to see how her behavior and stubbornness had hurt her and everyone around her.

One thing was for certain. There was no way I was going to reach out to her. Not for a good, long while.

A couple of weeks went by. One of my Reiki classmates had organized a weekly distance Reiki share. Since then, once a week, each of us got in contact with our partner (a different one was assigned each week) by phone, text, or email to set up a time to send and receive Reiki.

I looked forward to this because, in addition to receiving weekly treatment, it gave me the opportunity to practice and get feedback from my partner. On this particular week, my partner was Aimee, and I had asked her via text to please focus on my right biceps and general wellness. I didn't mention anything about my mom. In fact, I didn't mention anything personal at all.

Afterward, Aimee texted me and told me that while she was sending Reiki to me, she had received a message. It was the same three words, over and over: "Forgive your mother."

At this point, I should clarify that Aimee and I were only acquaintances, and we had only ever interacted at Reiki classes. We'd never talked about our personal issues before. Very few people knew about the fight with Mom, and I certainly hadn't posted anything about it on social media. Still, the message came through. It seemed the universe was trying to inject some love and understanding into our relationship.

Over the next few weeks, I made a conscious effort to lighten my heart with regard to Mom. I tried to focus on her good qualities instead of the hurt. I tried to focus on the fact that she is a good albeit troubled person who loves her kids very much.

Not long after, Mom called me out of the blue to say hello, acting like the fight had never happened. I was kind to her, but I let her know in no uncertain terms how much she had hurt Misha and me. I tried to guide the conversation toward how much she deserved to be happy instead of what I thought she needed to change.

Hopefully, it did her some good. It certainly helped me come closer to forgiving her.

72: VISITATIONS FROM THE BOBO

After Tyson's passing, we experienced several occurrences that left us confident we had experienced visitations from him. The first one happened to Misha. She was in the master bathroom when she heard what sounded like a muffled dog bark coming from somewhere near the living room. When she came out to investigate, she found Chloe fast asleep in her crate, which was situated in the hallway leading to the living room. While Misha thought it was possible Chloe had barked in her sleep, the bark didn't sound like Chloe's. It sounded like Tyson's. To this day, Misha believes Tyson paid her a visit that day.

The exact same thing happened again another time. Misha was again in the master bathroom when she heard a muffled dog bark that sounded just like Tyson. Once again, she came out to investigate to find Chloe asleep in her crate. This time, Madison was in the loft just above where Chloe was sleeping, but she didn't hear anything. Misha believes that this also was a visitation from Tyson.

One night after everyone had gone to bed, Madison was in her bed with Chloe when she woke to the sounds of something rustling through food packaging in the kitchen. She was certain Tyson was in there, mischievously stealing food. Although there were no physical signs to indicate any food had been disturbed, Lisa Silverman told me on several occasions that Tyson spent a lot of time in our kitchen.

And then it happened to me. I was in the kitchen when I heard a muffled dog bark coming from the hallway. It sounded exactly like Tyson. When I checked, Chloe was asleep in her crate. As with Misha's experiences, I reasoned that it could have been Chloe barking in her sleep—but still, if I had to bet my pension, I'd say it sounded a lot more like Tyson than Chloe.

The next time something happened to me, I was sleeping. I was in a strange state—not a restful one. I wasn't dreaming, yet I was very much aware of my surroundings. I've since described this to several people, and most of them have had similar experiences.

Suddenly, I became aware of a presence other than that of Misha or Madison or even Chloe. I couldn't read its intentions; they were ambiguous. From my sleep state, I told the presence that if it had positive intentions, it was welcome to stay. But if its intentions were negative, it needed to get lost.

It was at this point that I began to experience mild electrical impulses throughout my body. They were significantly stronger than what I feel in my hands when I channel Reiki. It was nothing at all like being shocked, and it was certainly not painful. If anything, it was oddly pleasant.

After a couple of seconds, the sensation intensified tenfold. It was like being electrocuted, but there was no sensation of pain. Again, it felt strangely pleasant. I knew instinctively that it was coming from a positive source, but I had no idea what the source was or why I was receiving it. The pulse of energy continued for about ten seconds, then it was gone.

When I woke the next morning, I recalled the incident and thought to myself how crazy it all felt. I wasn't afraid, but I was a bit concerned that if I told Misha and Madison about it, it might scare them. To this point, they'd both been hugely supportive of my metaphysical pursuits, but I wasn't confident that they'd receive this information with the same openness. I decided not to worry about it for the time being and kept it to myself.

The next day was a tiring one, and I was burned out and weary by the end of it. As I got into bed, Misha and Chloe were already asleep, cuddling. Our bedroom door was closed, and Madison was in the loft on the other side of the house. As I pulled the covers over me, I heard what sounded like Tyson barking outside the bedroom door. Not once or twice, but three times.

I wondered if I was hearing things. I double-checked to make sure Chloe was, in fact, in bed with us. When I saw that she was, I felt positive that Tyson had just paid us a visit. Still, I made a mental note to ask Madison in the morning if she'd heard what I did.

I fell asleep quickly, but the rest didn't last long. About an hour later, I found myself in that same strange sleep state: consciously aware, but not dreaming. At that very instant, I heard Tyson's bark in my left ear. This time it was a very physical sensation, and it felt as if he'd been no more than an inch away from my head.

I jolted upright, looking around for him. I reached for Chloe and found her fast asleep down near my right thigh. The Bobo had obviously stopped by to say hi. I giggled as I fell back asleep, knowing that The Asshole of Love was still very much with us.

I was so thankful he had made the effort to reach out to me in such an up-close and personal way rather than having to hear it secondhand from Misha. It did my heart a whole lot of good.

The next time I spoke to her, Lisa confirmed for me that all of the visitations we'd experienced had been Tyson. She also told me that the "electrocution" had been necessary to raise my energy vibration to a level where Tyson would be able to communicate with me.

That August, we took a vacation to Hawaii. Aunt Pam house-sat for us, taking care of Chloe and our chinchilla, Skipper Dee. Pam had stayed with Tyson and Chloe several times before, and they had always seemed to enjoy her presence.

A few days into the trip, when I called Pam to check on her, she asked me a very strange question. "Does Chloe have a bad leg like Tyson had?"

This was concerning to hear, as Chloe had always been very strong and healthy with no known ailments. "No," I said. "Why do you ask?"

"Well," Pam said, "all of a sudden, Chloe started walking around, holding her right rear leg up just like Tyson used to."

"I've never seen her do that before," I told her. "Is she still doing it? I wonder if she hurt herself."

"No, she isn't. She only did it for a little while yesterday, and she hasn't done it since."

You don't have to be a mind reader to guess what went through my head. I thought maybe Tyson was paying Pam a visit, letting her know he was still with her, too.

"I wonder if Tyson was visiting you," I said, to which she replied:

"That's kinda what I was thinking."

I told Pam that we were pretty sure he had visited us on several occasions, and that he must be very fond of her to do that. "That's quite an honor," I said. "Not too many people were lucky enough to be a part of Tyson's inner circle."

Pam laughed, but I could tell she was taking it as seriously as I was. It appeared our boy was making a real effort to let us know he still loved and watched over us.

73: ALONG CAME ELLIE

While we were in Hawaii, I received a phone call from my sister, Andrea. We chatted for a while. I told her all about our vacation, and she told me how things were going with her family's recent move to Prescott, Arizona.

Then, in a regretful tone, she hit me with the news. "Mom got a puppy."

For most people, this would be exciting news, but Mom had absolutely no business getting a puppy.

A few years before, a lifetime of smoking had caught up to her and she'd had a massive heart attack and a stroke. This left her physically disabled. She wasn't exactly paralyzed, but her coordination became significantly diminished.

As a result, she'd fallen a few times, resulting in multiple overnight trips to the hospital. Her condition made it difficult, even dangerous, for her to walk a dog, let alone a puppy—so when Andrea told me that the puppy was a mini Goldendoodle (a Poodle/Golden Retriever mix) capable of pulling her to the ground, all I could do was shake my head and laugh.

I knew Mom wasn't going to be able to properly care for the pup, which wasn't right. This was typical of Mom. Over the years since the divorce, she'd purchased seven different homes, at least seven different cars, and had seven different dogs—not counting the new puppy or Sox, who she had "taken for a ride" during my sophomore year of high school.

Mom still had one of these dogs, a little white Maltese named Snowy, so why had she gotten yet another dog, especially one she couldn't even care for? Getting new houses, cars, and dogs was her way of injecting some excitement into her life and distracting her from her unhappiness. I know this sounds harsh, but it was the truth. Because she no longer had the financial means to buy a new home and she could no longer drive, dogs had become her go-to.

"I wish I could say I'm surprised," I said.

"Oh, Mom," Andrea sighed. This was a saying she'd uttered countless times over the years whenever Mom made a bad decision or lashed out at one of us.

"So, how long do you think it'll be before the puppy trips her or something and she falls on her face?" I asked.

"Probably not very long. We were thinking maybe you'd be willing to take the puppy?"

Mom's health issues had severely burdened Andrea, her husband Chris, and Chris's parents over the years, both financially and time-wise. I wanted to do my part, but I didn't think we were ready for a new dog yet.

Unless, of course, the dog was Tyson.

Still, I wasn't about to say no. Besides, I didn't want the puppy to end up in foster care or in a shelter.

"When the time comes, give me a call. I'm sure we can work something out," I assured her.

In the space of two weeks, Mom tripped over the puppy numerous times and broke her wrist. I was surprised when Mom herself called and asked me to adopt the dog, but I guess being laid up in an in-patient rehabilitation facility has a way of making someone see reality.

I had her on speakerphone at the time so Misha could listen in. She shook her head in disgust and mouthed the words, "Damn it!"

I told Mom I would get back to her in a couple of days so that I could discuss it with Misha and Madison. I also wanted to see if I could arrange a consultation with Sondy to check in with the puppy herself. For all I knew, she had another path in mind. I also wanted to see how Chloe felt about it, as she seemed to enjoy being an "only" dog.

Fortunately, Sondy was able to squeeze me in the next afternoon. I told her the situation, and she was able to connect with both the puppy and Chloe. The puppy communicated that, while she felt cared for by Mom, her living space was too small and she didn't get to run around enough. Mind you, I hadn't told Sondy anything about Mom's home, a one-bedroom condominium.

During the session, the puppy also indicated that, while she felt Mom liked her, she didn't sense that their connection would be long-term. She also said she wanted to live in a home with a child. When Sondy offered her a chance to be adopted by us, she accepted.

Sondy communicated to me that the puppy wanted to be named

Ellie and that she had an incredibly positive energy about her that would bring a lot of joy to our home. Later, Sondy advised me that Ellie means "shining light."

Although Chloe admitted she was enjoying her time as an only dog, she was excited about the prospect of having a friend to play with, saying, "I get to have a playmate?!" in response to Sondy's offer of the puppy coming to live with us.

I also took the opportunity to check in with Tyson, who, as always, was right there with us. I had Sondy ask him whether he'd be coming back soon. While he was noncommittal as usual, Sondy got the distinct impression he would be coming back before long. He communicated to Sondy that he'd been in communication with Ellie in the spiritual realm and that he had actually helped orchestrate her coming to us.

Tyson was very excited to hear we'd decided to adopt Ellie, and he communicated this by sending Sondy an image of a person sitting in a chair with the head of Disney's Cheshire Cat.

With fascination, Sondy abruptly advised me that Tyson had sent her the image of him in a Superman suit. This was remarkable because, as I mentioned earlier, Tyson did, in fact, wear a Superman suit.

Even with all of the astounding experiences I'd had over the previous year and a half, I still possessed a healthy level of skepticism, so this piece of information—which was nothing Sondy could have known about—was very affirming.

Tyson went on to communicate that he was helping to facilitate my ability with Reiki, as well as with writing this book. This came as no surprise. After all, Lisa, Sondy, Anna, and Aumara had all told me that he was close to me. It only made sense that he would be helping me to write our story, as well as helping me with Reiki.

Tyson also told Sondy that he wanted the book to be dedicated to "The spirit of love for animals, or something similar." This would be a worthy dedication, indeed.

After the session with Sondy, I called Misha and told her all about it. We had decided that if Chloe and the puppy, now known as Ellie, gave us the green light, we would adopt her—so with reluctance in her voice, Misha said, "Okay, go down there and get her."

The drive to Phoenix would take me eleven hours if I only stopped for gas, and the only time I had available to go was the following week. I got a day off of work and made reservations for a rental car. Everything was set. Then the phone rang. It was Andrea. She was calling to tell me that Mom had decided she no longer wanted to give Ellie up.

As I'm sure you can imagine, I wasn't too happy. I was also sure it was only a matter of time before Mom fell on her face again. To make things worse, Misha and I had by now embraced the idea of the new addition to our family, and so had Madison. She was going to be very disappointed.

I asked Andrea to tell Mom this was a one-chance deal; that I was still planning on coming to get Ellie, but if she decided to keep her, we wouldn't adopt her in the future. I wasn't about to have my family placed on an emotional yo-yo.

A couple of days before I was scheduled to leave for Arizona, Mom had a change of heart. She called and told me that she wanted us to adopt Ellie. She seemed to have accepted it was the best thing for both her and the pup, and I assured her Ellie would have a good life with us. Plus, I told Mom, she could visit her any time she wanted. She seemed to be at peace with it.

The whirlwind trip to pick up Ellie went remarkably smoothly. I left first thing on Monday morning and was back home by Wednesday afternoon. Ellie turned out to be exactly as Sondy described her. She had the happiest, most positive energy I could have imagined. She was a total lover. She was also very smart. It only took a few minutes to teach her to sit, come, and stay.

What didn't seem to jibe with what Sondy had said was that Chloe didn't seem to want anything to do with her. Being a puppy of only four months, all Ellie wanted to do was play. She was constantly up in Chloe's grill, and Chloe wasn't pleased at all. She'd bare her teeth and scream, which only seemed to egg Ellie on. Oddly, Skipper Dee took to Ellie instantly, constantly trying to play "kissy-face" with her.

I sent Sondy an email letting her know how things were progressing with Ellie. She wasn't terribly surprised by Chloe's reaction, as she was almost nine, and adjusting to puppy energy can be difficult for older dogs.

Once, I asked Sondy if animals sometimes communicated with her when she wasn't in a session with a client. She said that, for the most part, they only came through when she was making an effort to "tune in" to them during a session. This made it all the more unusual and intriguing when she informed me that ever since our last session two weeks prior, Tyson had been periodically sending her an image of him in the Superman suit.

According to Sondy, Tyson was adamant that I use this image for the cover of the book. But the travesty was that, as far as I knew, we didn't have any photos of him in the suit. I decided we would simply have to figure something out.

74: TYSON'S GIFT

I pored over all of our photo albums to find a picture of Tyson in the Superman suit. Nothing. I couldn't believe we'd been so blind as to overlook such a ridiculously cute photo opportunity. Unfortunately, back when he'd worn the suit around 2005, smartphones weren't a thing—and who walked around with a camera at the ready? Not me.

The more I thought of Tyson being represented as a superhero, the more emotional I became. I felt so much love, pride, and appreciation for Tyson and the way he'd touched our lives, the way he'd touched my soul. He healed my heart in a way only he could; he gave me a friendship and connection only he could. He helped Misha and me grow closer in a way only he could. He made me earn it in a way only he could. And he provided us with a lifetime of memories that only he could.

From the time he came into our lives, we knew he was special and that we should appreciate every moment with him. I also knew that when we inevitably lost him, I would be devastated. Still, I never could have predicted the incredible spiritual growth it would spark in me. I never could have predicted that losing him would open me up to a whole new, beautiful metaphysical world. I never could have predicted that my furry little soul mate would be by my side, helping me grow and heal as much in death as he had in life. Perhaps most importantly, I never could have predicted he would show me that we live on after our physical death; that our love lives on; that we are eternal souls having an earthly experience. He was my best friend.

Not long ago, Misha and I took a walk on the beach. We talked about Tyson's life and the beautiful impact he'd on us all.

"What an amazing gift," I said.

"There's your title," Misha replied.

"What do you mean?"

"*Tyson's Gift.* That's your title."

I'd been working on the book for a while but hadn't put any thought into what the title would be. Now, hearing Misha's words, it felt so fitting and reverent. I couldn't help the tears that fell. I felt that same shot of love, pride, and appreciation I'd felt when I imagined him as Super Tyson.

I knew that she was right. It was perfect.

EPILOGUE

I never found a picture of Tyson in the Superman suit, so I decided to get creative. Frankly, I think it is a much better choice—and according to Sondy, Tyson approves.

I've continued to practice Reiki, and I'm now a certified Reiki Master, which means I can teach it as well as practice it. I believe I will do so for the rest of my life. After all, it's hard to imagine such a gift being given only to be wasted.

It is my sincere and humble hope that this book will inspire others with even a small amount of the hope and peace the experiences within its pages provided and continue to provide me. I think that most everyone who has ever had a loved pet, whether a dog, cat, bird, or chinchilla, can relate to the joy and love Tyson brought to our lives. Hopefully, that alone made it worth reading.

I also hope that the more metaphysical aspects of our story will offer hope and peace to those in need of it. For those who are skeptical, I get it. I really do. And I don't blame you one bit. However, I encourage you to do your own exploring, whether it be through reading or seeking out your own session with a credible spiritual medium.

Believe me, there's a big difference between reading about it and experiencing it for yourself. There are many, many books on this type of subject matter containing thousands of case studies, the credibility of which are hard to deny if one examines them with an open mind. *Many Lives, Many Masters* by Brian Weiss, M.D., or *Journey of Souls* by Michael Newton, Ph.D., are great places to start. I'd also recommend *Talking to Heaven* by James Van Praagh or *The Spirit Whisperer* by John Holland. Of course *The Boy Who Knew Too Much* by Cathy Byrd and *Animals and The Afterlife* by Kim Sheridan are also great books.

Frankly, there's so much material out there, it's hard to believe that metaphysical occurrences are generally looked upon with such skepticism. And, of course, I say that as someone who knows all about skepticism.

For those who have any interest in Reiki, do yourself a favor and seek out a class. Like I said, it doesn't take any special ability to do it. All it takes is the openness and desire to help others. There is nothing to be afraid of. It will only bring love and peace to your life!

Will there be a book two? That all depends on Tyson. If he comes back, I will most definitely tell the story. I don't know if or when, but I believe he will. When he's ready, he will.

Until then, I wish you peace and happiness.

Brandon Wainwright
December 30, 2019

AFTERWORD

In February of 2020, we were on vacation in Maui when Misha got a text from her close friend Donna. Donna had done a trial adoption of a Chihuahua named Mindy. She had hoped to adopt Mindy so her other dog, Vinnie, would have a companion, but the two didn't jibe.

Donna said that Mindy was very sweet and super cute and reminded her of Tyson. Then she sent us a photo of Mindy.

Being well aware of our belief that Tyson would come back to us, Donna asked, "Do you think she could be Tyson?"

She then gave us the link to the dog rescue's adoption application in case we were interested in meeting Mindy.

Mindy's resemblance to Tyson was undeniable. Her coloring and ears were different, but otherwise, she was very similar, especially the intelligence in her eyes. And yes, she was indeed *super* cute!

I was excited about the prospect of bringing this sweet little girl into our lives, but I wasn't about to get my hopes up that an adoption would even work out since we wouldn't be home for almost a week. While I was open to the idea that Mindy could be the reincarnation of Tyson, I was skeptical. I had gotten used to the idea that it would probably be a while before he returned.

Ever since Tyson had passed, I had occasionally gone on the local animal rescue websites to look at their dogs. I did this partly because I enjoyed looking at the dogs, but secretly I was hoping I would spot the reincarnated Tyson. There had been one little Chihuahua mix I thought had potential, but he was adopted before I could even fill out an application. Misha wasn't a fan of my perusal of the rescue websites. She thought I was torturing myself, but I insisted I was simply keeping my eyes peeled.

Now, sensing the excitement in Misha's voice, I shook my head. "Oh, sure, when *Donna* suggests a dog might be Tyson, you're all in. When *I* suggest it, I'm torturing myself."

"It's just that this is how Tyson came into our lives the first time," she reasoned. "He just came out of the blue, without us seeking him out."

She definitely had a point. I pulled out my iPad and filled out the online application for Mindy right there by the pool. That night, I got an email from Lynn, the rescue director, who said she very much liked our application and would forward it to Mindy's foster parents to facilitate setting up an in-person meeting as soon as we were back in town.

Misha and I were excited and surprised; we thought Mindy would have been adopted before we could return. We certainly didn't expect that they would be willing to hold her for us.

We went back to enjoying Maui, with little Mindy always in the back of our minds. Would she be joining our family? Was she, in fact, Tyson, back so soon in female form? We would know before long.

ADDENDUM (November 2020)

As we close in on the publication of *Tyson's Gift*, I want to give a brief update on Mindy. In short, Mindy *is* Tyson. Actually, I should say "Pepper" is Tyson. We felt that was a much more suitable name and decided on that. (Yes, Pepper is every bit as spicy as Tyson!)

There are many reasons to believe this, not the least of which are her personality and certain key physical characteristics. Additionally, I've received confirmation from Lisa, Aumara, Sondy, and other intuitives.

I knew instinctively that Pepper was Tyson within a few days of having her. Sure, I had to break through some healthy skepticism, but I knew it through and through. There will most certainly be a second book, and I look forward to sharing our story with you.

ACKNOWLEDGMENTS

First, I'd like to thank Misha and Madison Wainwright for being supportive and loving through this whole process. I'm sure in the beginning, you both thought my spiritual exploration was a bit odd, but you were steadfast, nonetheless.

My deepest gratitude goes to Sondy Kaska, Lisa Silverman, and Melinda Leslie for your intuitive talents and guidance. You've helped open me up to a whole new spiritual world. Sondy can be found at heartgemscommunication.com, Lisa at decoratorguru.com, and Melinda at sedonanewagestore.com/psychics/Melinda.

To Anna Dorian, my amazing Reiki teacher, I want you to know that your talents both as a teacher and Reiki practitioner helped me to "get it" on both an intellectual and spiritual level. Also, thank you for being the first catalyst in the creation of this book.

To Mike and Chellie Kammermeyer, who are also my dear Reiki teachers, thank you for helping me to expand my understanding and relationship with Reiki. Learn more at innercompassreiki.com.

To Aumara Bonnet, you have been an amazing source of guidance and light. Thank you for giving me the spiritual push I needed to start writing this book despite my doubts. I'm so thankful our paths have crossed. Visit her at teachingsofdivineoneness.com.

A big shout out to Vince Font of Glass Spider Publishing. You've been invaluable in making this book the best it could be. I truly believe I was guided to you, and I'll always be thankful I kept searching for the right publisher, even when I had other offers.

To the men and women of law enforcement, your integrity and dedication to our communities is remarkable. Thank you for helping me to become the person I am.

To my soulmate and spiritual co-author, Tyson, thank you for guiding me with so much love and dedication. You are my heartlight.

Finally, I give my humble appreciation to God. Thank you for everything.

ABOUT THE AUTHOR

Brandon Wainwright is a police officer and Reiki practitioner in the San Francisco Bay Area, where he lives with his wife, daughter, two dogs, and a chinchilla.

Made in United States
North Haven, CT
31 August 2022

23537161R00114